LOVE BETTER SOONER

Learning the Art of Intentional Love

To Chelsea —
A survivor of love,

Mark Ben...

by

Mark Benish
with Tricia Heyer

Love Better Sooner

Copyright © 2018 by Mark Benish

The views and opinions expressed in this book are those of the author and do not necessarily reflect the official policy or position or Illumify Media Global.

Scripture quotations are taken from Holy Bible, New International Version®, NIV® Copyright ©1973, 1978, 1984, 2011 by Biblica, Inc.® Used by permission. All rights reserved worldwide.

All names in this book have been changed for the sake of privacy.

Paperback ISBN: 978-1-947360-16-7
eBook ISBN: 978-1-947360-17-4

Printed in the United States of America

CONTENTS

For all who have loved me:
you taught me with your love.

And especially for Cindy,
who teaches me with her love every day.

Foreword

ALMOST THIRTY YEARS AGO, I fell in love with Mark's wisdom.

We attended the same church for many years, and shortly after my first marriage ended, I was working through a lonely season of a broken heart. Sunday mornings were very difficult for me, and I often cried my way through worship and communion.

One Sunday morning, after church, Mark came up to me, put his hand on my shoulder, and said, "You look like you're having a really hard time. If you ever need someone to talk to, feel free to call me."

On a late night a few weeks later, when I was feeling especially lonely, I remembered his invitation. I called him at eleven o'clock that night and talked to him for an hour or two. I did this quite a lot, actually, after that initial call. What I didn't know then about Mark is that he owned a restaurant and worked a jillion hours a week, and he generally preferred to go to bed around nine thirty! But I needed someone to talk to, and he put himself out there for me, though he was likely falling asleep on the other end of the phone line.

We kept talking on the phone, sort of phone "dating," and as we got to know one another, Mark built me up so much. He lifted me up and made me feel I was a worthy person. He came to love me the way I was, not trying to change me, but just being there to help me if I wanted help or needed to make a change. He was a strong support, endorsing who I was as a person.

Many months (and *many* phone calls) later, when we were folding laundry together one evening, we decided we wanted to keep folding laundry together, to build a life together. A little over a year after that first phone call, we were married in that church we attended together. The journey of loving this man, of being loved by him, has been one of the greatest journeys of my life.

As I said, I fell in love with Mark's wisdom. And I fell in love with *him* because he was a listener. He was willing to help me if I needed it, but he was also willing to love me where I was. That's who Mark is in our marriage together, it's who he is in his counseling practice, and it's who he is in the pages of this book. He's willing to listen, to share what he knows, to help you move forward if you want to, and to appreciate exactly where you are.

I am so happy to share my husband with you.

—Cindy Benish

Introduction

LET'S DIVE RIGHT IN and begin with a story I'm not proud of. My wife and I were celebrating our twentieth anniversary, and we had planned a February trip to Phoenix to golf together. The golf courses were immaculate, and the weather was perfect every single day, with sunny days stretching into the seventies.

On the third morning of our trip, we were off to another great start, and we were even fortunate to be paired with a great couple for our eighteen holes. Cindy beat me on the front nine, and let me say, she had never beat me on nine holes before. She was lighthearted and carefree for the rest of the day. Our scores were low, and our spirits were high. Perfect weather, great golfing, new friends, delightful conversation, endless hours with my wife . . . it was a recipe of greatness. (The golfer in me wants you to know that I did manage to win the match, just for the record!)

We went to dinner that night at a fabulous Italian restaurant, complete with a delicious meal and an expensive bottle of wine. As we walked across the parking lot after dinner, I had one thing on my mind: all the goodness the evening held for us. I had big plans for my bride. I knew we'd go back to the condo we'd rented, make love, and celebrate an absolutely perfect day together.

We got in the car, I put the car in reverse, and I said, "Okay, how do we find the condo?"

Now, Cindy is a highly intelligent woman. She is good at so many things, and I'm eager to tell you about those in the coming chapters. But navigation is not one of her gifts. Compass directions and GPS instructions do not mesh well with her very smart mind. She has memories from before we were together when a driver wanted instructions and navigational turns faster than she could provide them back in the day when maps were enormous tricks of origami, folded every which way. Those memories are unpleasant for good reasons, and she hates to revisit them. I know this about her, but in my haste to get started with our after-dinner plans, I didn't even give her enough time for the GPS to boot up all the way before I was demanding to know where to go. I triggered her emotions in a big way.

I was impatient with Cindy because I knew that if I made a wrong turn, I'd appear incompetent. (I *hate* to appear incompetent.) So, I was demeaning to her, and I was a jerk. Naturally, she reacted negatively—she was a jerk right back. (She says she wasn't. I remember it differently.) And just like that, all of our after-dinner plans circled the drain of the glorious evening. We got back to the condo, and there was an ice-cold crevasse right down the middle of that anniversary bed.

Do you ever wish you could go back and do something over again? I wished for a second chance on that night of our anniversary trip, but if I'm honest with you, I have wished that over a number of seasons of my life. I wish I had learned to love better, sooner. It's the bottom line and the absolute truth.

We had a night of loneliness to let the ice between us thaw a bit, and I'm glad to tell you, we recovered the next morning. I apologized to her for being a total jerk and belittling her, and she apologized for responding in kind. That mistake did not define our anniversary weekend. If you were to talk to Cindy today, she would tell you what a wonderful trip it was. That fight could be a forgotten footnote in the history of our marriage, except that it has taken root in my mind, reminding me of a shameful time when I exacerbated the wounds my wife already had. I cut her heart into slivers anytime I act this way, and I hate when I do that. My wife is the second-best gift God has given to me, second only to the promise of eternity with Him as my Savior. While I shouldn't put her on a pedestal, I should definitely treat her as the most important gift in my world. But frequently, I treat her with far less esteem than she deserves.

I learned a lot on that fateful night and the morning after. I can clearly see now that there is a truth that I want to keep at the front and center of every argument:

No issue is more important than how I am loving my wife. I need to be filled up, charged up, and energized by the desire to love her well.

I understand that when I am sarcastic or condescending to my wife, I am slicing and dicing her heart and the soul of who she is, and I don't want to do that anymore. I don't want there to be any separation in our marriage, and certainly not any distance that I've caused. I want us to always get stronger, to love more deeply, and to move closer to one another. My focus must be to equip, empower, and enable her to become all the woman that God intended her to be.

In the years since that Arizona night, I have been committed to not being sarcastic or demeaning to my wife, ever again. I wish I could tell you that I haven't hurt her a single time since, but sadly, that's not the case. But I am a whole lot better than I was five years ago. In fact, we have both improved in the intervening years, and now, when separation creeps in, we cut it off sooner. We recover more quickly. We are more intentional about strengthening the bonds of our relationship as soon as possible.

I'm still learning. I want to do better, be better, love better. And I want you to do the same. Ultimately, that's why I wrote this book. I want to empower you to learn from my mistakes. I have penned these pages with a heart desire to help you in three ways:

- to give you hope that your marriage can be something different, something better

- to give you the tools to put change into effect

- to free you from regrets for not having learned to love better sooner

Let's Start the Journey

One of my favorite movies is *Apollo 13*. The film came out in the mid-1990s, and it tells the story of the three astronauts aboard Apollo 13 for America's third moon landing mission in 1970. While they are en route to the moon, an explosion on board deprives their spacecraft of most of their oxygen supply and electric power—the very resources they need to survive at all, let alone get to the moon and back home again. NASA's flight controllers decide to abort the mission, and instead they begin an epic battle to get the three men home safely. Every time I watch the film, I'm struck by the complexity of the rescue as the team of aerospace engineers on the ground work so tirelessly to bring the astronauts home.

They're in the middle of the crisis, working against the clock, and nothing is going the way they planned. Gene Kranz, the flight director, grows more and more frustrated, as it looks like NASA's best efforts can only get the astronauts halfway home. He draws a graph on the chalkboard in their lab, indicating where Apollo 13 is and where home is and shows that their proposed solutions are so far insufficient and will only get the command module halfway home. "We're going to have to figure it out," he says at last. "I want this mark all the way back to Earth with time to spare. We never lost an American in space. We're . . . not gonna lose one on my watch. *Failure is not an option.*"[1]

Perhaps you feel as if you're living a version of the Apollo 13 story. Maybe your marriage isn't going the way you had planned. You may feel that you're far from where you want to be, and your best efforts will only get you halfway home. Or maybe you're not even sure what "home" looks like anymore. May I paint that vision for you?

Within marriage, "home" isn't a place. It's a feeling, a blend of peace, contentment, and joy. They build on one another. Increased peace in the marriage leads to contentment, which ultimately produces joy. How can we cultivate such a blend? What's more, how can we get to a place where we each think of our partner as our beloved, as a teammate, lover, friend, and maybe most important, a confidant? It happens through trust, and this book is about building trust in marriage by learning to serve, delight, sacrifice for, heal, and choose vulnerability with that important person with whom you've chosen to live the big and small moments of your life.

I want you to know, I'm here to partner with you. This mission—your marriage—isn't going down on my watch. I want to help you in every way I can, to bring you to growth, healing, and intimacy in a thriving marriage.

Welcome to my practice. Let's get you home safely.

TOOL FOR THE JOURNEY:

I need to be filled up, charged up, and energized by the desire to love my partner well.

PART ONE

How Did We Get Here?

Know Your GPS

WHY IN THE WORLD don't I treat my beloved *as my beloved?* At times, I shower Cindy with all the honor and respect I can muster, and other times I'm horrible and insulting to her. I've been closely involved with so many couples, both through financial coaching and marriage counseling, and I've discovered that their patterns are like mine. As I look at my own life and compare my failed first marriage with my strong and intimate marriage with Cindy, I am surprised that there are still times when I find myself doing exactly what I didn't do right the first time. Sometimes, we still struggle.

We like to think that we are rational beings and that our logic and intelligence drive our decisions. But if each of us wants to love well, if we intend to do the right thing, then logic would imply that we simply *would* do the right thing. If that were the case, marriage counselors all over the country would give up their practices because people would simply *know* what to do to love well—and do it. But you and I both know that's not the case. Marriages are still struggling, and divorce rates are at an all-time high. And so, it must not be our thoughtful understanding and awareness that drive the way we relate to one another. If it is not our rationality, then what drives us?

In part 1, I will share with you the model I've developed to answer those questions. I will also help you make a discovery. While you thought you were attracted to your beloved for reasons well within your choosing and control, I propose that there were some hidden factors deep at work. Let me pull back the curtain and give you a different framework to see what's really going on.

TOOLS FOR THE JOURNEY

The pastor of the church where I came to Christ in my twenties used to say that it's hard to understand new concepts unless you have hooks on the wall where you can hang something new that you're learning. We need a place to put new things. Our brains crave organization, and we function best when we know where to find our tools—both physically and metaphorically.

I picture it as resembling a pegboard over the workbench in a garage or a carpenter's studio. You could simply pile all your tools on the workbench, but then it's hard to find them when you need them. If you can't find your tools, you can't use them. Instead, if you post hooks into a pegboard, then you can organize the space, you know where to store things, and you can find something when you need it.

In the chapters to come, five crucial practices will become our five hooks. We can hang our behaviors on these hooks of awareness, and we can come back to them when it's time to put them into practice. We will discuss these "hooks" in part 2.

I have woven these chapters with stories of marriages and family relationships, and I've carefully chosen each as an example—sometimes of what to do, and sometimes of what *not* to do. I invite you into the conversations with my clients and with my wife to see these five practices unfolding in action.

Each chapter contains a tool for your marriage, a takeaway that you can begin to use and apply immediately. You'll also find exercises for further thoughts and conversation. The "Think About" section invites you to do a personal inventory in response to the themes of the chapter, and the "Talk About" section allows you to deepen your understanding by sharing what you've discovered with your beloved, learning his or her perspective, and deepening your experience together.

Caution: There May Be Hazards Ahead

The conversations, exercises, and tools are designed to be a manual for you to return to as you and your loved one shape your relationship together, and they are designed to help you communicate. However, some questions can be difficult for couples to talk about, and some topics may cause conflict between the two of you. If the exercises are not helping you communicate better, *don't do them.* Skip them. The questions are not the point.

I want to equip you to love one another better, and if any of the questions cause tension, confrontation, or harm, seriously, just don't do them. I want to help you, not harm you, and so I invite you to do what is best for the two of *you.*

There. I think now we've laid all the groundwork, and I am so eager to get started with you. Thank you for letting me walk this path alongside you.

CHAPTER ONE

Welcome to My Practice
Tools for the Journey

I WASN'T ALWAYS A marriage counselor. In fact, I owned and operated a Chick-fil-A for many years. (A special nod to waffle fries and Sundays off.) After decades of running my own business, on track to early retirement with a solid nest egg, Cindy and I sold the restaurant, sold our home, and relocated from California to Colorado in pursuit of a new calling on my life: graduate school and a career in marriage counseling. Our friends told us what a brave thing we were doing, but it didn't feel like a great feat of courage to us. We had a clear sense of a call from God, so we headed on our way.

We had made the decision long ago to live a debt-free life, and I believe that freed us to be available to hear this new calling on our lives. If we had had a huge car payment, a boat payment, a credit card balance, and no money in the bank, I don't think we would have been in a place to hear with such clarity and to say yes. Still, to step away from my career in my midfifties, to commit to three years with no income? Well, in terms of retirement planning, you could say that's a formula for financial disaster.

I was up to my eyeballs in going to graduate school thirty years after college. I was beginning the second act of my life, but I was surrounded by bright-eyed thinkers with young families, big dreams, and a whole path ahead of them. I remember when I went to the library for the first time. I asked one of my colleagues (who was half my age) to point me to the card catalog. "See that computer over there?" he said. " Things have changed."

My undergraduate degree was in business, where writing anything more than a page was considered too wordy. But in seminary, on the first day of class, the professor said, "Okay, next week I'd like for you to write five pages on this topic, and don't forget to include the theology."

F-f-five p-pages?? Th-th-th-theology?? What is that? I thought. *And what have I gotten myself into?*

The path was not easy. I graduated with two degrees in three years, and I wrote the equivalent of three books in that length of time. The journey depleted me in ways I could not have expected, and upon graduation, I found myself looking into the deep, black, bottomless hole of trying to find a job in a difficult economy. We had trusted the Lord with the move; we would need to keep trusting Him.

In time, I began to find my stride. I started a private practice. I see clients every day during the week, I speak at seminars on marriage and relationships, and I teach workshops on marriage and blending families on the weekends. I will say, I still have a lot of years in front of me before I'll be on the golf course every afternoon. We lost a lot of money, security, and freedom by taking this right turn so late in life, but neither of us would say we regret it. It's only been a blessing. God was clear to each of us that it was time to make the move, and He has been faithful to us through every turn and every day. I can trust Him with the retirement too.

One Big Question

After I graduated from seminary, I spent three years reading through the four Gospels: Matthew, Mark, Luke, and John. I recognize that the history of Jesus can be a hot button for some people, as the our varied views on whether He was the Savior of the world, a prophet, or simply a good guy span the spectrum. But regardless of how you feel about Jesus, we can agree on one thing: He lived out His greatest commandment.

As I focused exclusively on these four books of the Bible, I studied a number of different versions and translations. Everything pointed back to One Big Question: How did Jesus love? What in the world does that mean, anyway? I was looking for some practical examples to guide my daily life. Our culture is so confused about what love is and what it isn't, but I wanted to go straight to the source Himself.

Matthew told the story of when someone asked Jesus, "Teacher, what is the greatest commandment?"

> Jesus replied: "'Love the Lord your God with all your heart and with all your soul and with all your mind.' This is the first and greatest commandment. And the second is like it: 'Love your neighbor as yourself.' All the Law and the Prophets hang on these two commandments." (Matthew 22:36–40)

Essentially, Jesus named two equal commands. He said that we are to love God with everything we've got, and that we are to love others as we love ourselves. In my mind, I picture this as a three-legged stool: I need to learn to love God with everything I've got, love myself with everything I've got, and love others with everything I've got. Without any one of these legs, the stool falls over. If you don't love God well, love others well, and love yourself well—the hardest one for us to do, by the way—then your stool falls over.

But these are not listed in a random order—they matter sequentially. Jesus said we are to love God first. That causes a lot of people to set Him aside in an invisible box labeled "Priority Number One." They put family in the box labeled "Priority Number Two," and they place work in the box labeled "Priority Number Three." We put things in boxes because we like things compartmentalized. But I don't think that's what Jesus is asking us to do.

I think He's saying that my entire life needs to be infused with my relationship with God. He doesn't want us to separate Him *apart from* everything we do—no, He wants to *be part of* everything we do. Not to simply put God first, but to invite Him into everything. An infusion. When my love for God is the lens through which I see my family, my friends, my work, and myself, then I can be much more loving—to everyone Jesus called me to love. He named this commandment as the most important calling of our lives, and the more we learn about Jesus, the more we will see that He consistently lived this out in every interaction of His life on earth.

Five Major Road Signs

I worked hard to wrap my mind around the notion and the command that I am supposed to love as Christ loved, and in my studying, I discovered five virtues that Jesus modeled in His interactions with people: sacrifice, delight, healing, vulnerability, and forgiveness. These are five major road signs that keep us on a path of loving intentionally.

The idea in this book is to focus on and expand these themes, developing them into five intentional practices to love well in marriage. These practices build on one another, and they overlap each other. While we will begin with one practice and then add another, please keep in mind that the journey is less like a linear path and more like a maze with many levels and twisting paths. Everything overlaps and affects everything else.

Some of the strengths I believe I bring to counseling are practical ways of thinking about these concepts, because marriage is truly about where the rubber meets the road. It's easy on Sunday to say, "Yes, of course, I love my wife." But what does that look like Monday through Saturday? Intentional love understands that how I treat my beloved—whether it is in the mundane moments of life, or when we disagree, or when we are tired, stressed, or unhappy—either kills love or feeds it. Intentional love focuses on connection, not separation.

Intentional love involves developing our conscious awareness of how we are treating others right now. *Right now* is when your marriage is unfolding, and how you treat your spouse *right now* can directly shape your life together. Intentional love can be the hallmark of your marriage.

Three Clients in Every Counseling Session

When a couple comes into my office, I realize I really have three clients: the husband, the wife, and the separate thing that is their marriage. I'm also very aware that—almost 100 percent of the time—one of them doesn't want to be there. Usually one-half of the marriage believes their marriage is "okay," while the other believes they're headed downward. One is waiting for me to decide who's right or wrong; the other is waiting to get a slap on the wrist or a punishment in the marriage time-out corner.

Perhaps that's true for you as you're reading this book. Maybe you are the one-half of the marriage who bought the book and wants something better for the two of you; or, maybe you are the other half, who isn't interested in another book about marriage. Because, let's be honest: there are a gazillion books about marriage. What makes this one different?

Let me tell you a few important things about my approach to marriage counseling. First, I don't do a lot of diagnosis. I don't like boxes, personality tests, and marriage assessments, because human beings are just too complex for formulas. This makes me a square peg in the round hole of counseling, but I stand firm with this approach.

Second, I do not play judge and jury with the couples who come into my office. I'm not going to decide if your wife needs to stay within budget or if your husband is irrational in the way he loads the dishwasher. There will always—*always*—be little arguments and challenges like these in your marriage, and you do not need a mediator to decide who is right or wrong. What you need most is the ability to love each other well while you're working through life's distractions and challenges, and this ability grows out of a relational process that is intentional.

I am well aware that God has *not* given me the wisdom of Solomon to know the details of your marital relationship. I do not have an all-knowing clairvoyance to understand what is happening at your dining room table and in your marriage bed. But I do believe He has given me wisdom about the process of healing a marriage and learning how to love each other better.

I believe that your marriage is a living, breathing entity. Just as a plant needs sunshine, air, soil, fertilizer, and water in order to thrive, a relationship also needs certain elements to survive. Your relationship needs conscious energy poured into it, and this comes with communication and awareness of one another—each of you as individuals, and the two of you together. Nothing will ever be more important than how well you love one another, and that comes down to how you treat each other on a daily basis.

TOOL FOR THE JOURNEY:

Intentional love can be the hallmark of our marriage. Intentional love involves developing our conscious awareness of how we are treating others right now. *Right now* is when our marriage is unfolding, and how I treat my spouse *right now* can directly shape our life together.

CHAPTER TWO

The First Fight
Clear Paths and Roadblocks

I'D LIKE FOR YOU to think with me about when you met your spouse. What initially caught your eye? What prompted that very first conversation? Go there in your mind, and picture those early, twitterpated days. Remember what she looked like? Remember how you felt about spending time together? Those early stages of infatuation offer an experience all their own. People have tried to bottle that emotion. It's a powerful drug, indeed.

While your story is beautifully yours and wonderfully personal, I'm sorry to tell you this: the story of how you met is not all that original. In fact, it's probably not unique at all. Try not to be offended. Stay with me here. I'm not saying your marriage is a cliché, but I am saying that relationships follow patterns. After thousands of hours with hundreds of couples, I have identified the patterns and stages on the path from "love at first sight" to "We've had our first fight" and beyond.

The first layer of a relationship is the *behavioral connection.* This is the moment when the other person does something that catches your attention. It may be her smile, his eyes, the engaging way he talks to the coffee barista, or the sway in her stride as she walks across the campus that first grabs you. We notice each other, and there is a flickering spark of interest. This is the moment when you find yourself thinking, *Well,* that's *interesting. I believe I'd like to know more.* There are elements that attract us, and these drive our energy to begin building a relationship.

Then we have the *cognitive connection.* As you begin conversation with this person, you're attracted to his or her mind. You begin to discover that this other person, to some degree, thinks about and sees the world the way you do, perhaps with a similar faith perspective or worldview. You have something in common. Of course, sometimes this is also where things first turn sour, when you might realize this person isn't like you at all.

In the years after my divorce, I was a single dad in the dating world. Dating is hard enough when you only have yourself to worry about, but when you have a child, the stakes are dramatically higher. I couldn't bring just anyone into the life my daughter and I shared. I needed to be with someone who could love my daughter, someone who understood the ups and downs of parenting, and someone who could partner with me on the journey of raising her well. I brought up the topic of parenting early on in those dating encounters, because I wanted to know where we stood before we got in too far. I could tell very soon if our parenting styles were very different, and my tendency was to run the other way. If I encountered a woman who was attractive, intelligent, and a great conversationalist, but then discovered she was defensive, reactive, and unwilling to engage in conversations about parenting, I wouldn't continue pursuing her. I learned quickly that the woman I was looking for would not be easy to find.

But then Cindy came into my life. Right away, I found her to be profoundly intelligent, an engaging conversationalist, beautiful, and a single parent to two of her own children. The parenting journey was her priority, too, and we had found a common denominator. Still, though we shared these nonnegotiable values, we found some bumps in the road that I've now come to know are pretty classic and common. (More to come on this tender topic.) Parenting is just one example of an area that matters to me. We all have our perspectives; you have yours, and I have mine. When we find these perspectives in common with someone else, we've just jumped another hurdle in building the relationship.

Next, you'll find you have an *emotional connection.* This is where we discover that we like to do a lot of the same things. You may have the same hobbies, or you enjoy reading the same kinds of books. When I do premarital counseling, couples just gush over one another and all of the things they love to do together. Oh, how they love to cook together and mountain bike and go bowling and watch birds. My, how they both love the Green Bay Packers, how they have a thing for American-made cars, and how they hate silent movies with subtitles. Whatever it is, you discover together that the same things make you happy. (I always leave one premarital session for six months after the wedding, when the couple usually tells me that there are actually a lot of things they really *don't* like to do together. But I digress. We'll get there later.)

Roadblock Ahead: The Emotional Barrier

Up until this point, the relationship has been growing closer and tighter on an emotional level. But every relationship will encounter the first fight, and that's when everything changes. There are things that matter deeply to each of us, things we keep hidden and protected. When someone gets too close, we put up a giant roadblock to protect ourselves and to keep the other person away. I call this the first *emotional barrier*, the fight that leads to emotional separation.

Take a moment to recall your first fight. What was it about? I'm willing to bet that somebody stepped on somebody else's feelings, and the other person reacted. Reactions are unique to each individual and can look any number of ways. One person may withdraw and give his or her partner the silent treatment. Another may get loud, angry, and verbal. Still another may make a dramatic exit, leaving the house, slamming the door, and squealing his or her tires while backing out of the driveway. You may start hurling insults, while your spouse may just give you the cold shoulder. We are emotional beings, and we react.

The first three stages of the relationship are pure fun, when you're flying high on pheromones and each other's presence. You're both wearing rose-colored glasses. But when you hit that first barrier, it's literally like the positive ends of magnets: you repel each other. In this stage of conflict, we are hard-wired to protect ourselves, to push away the person who has triggered a negative emotion in us. This is the emotional barrier.

Imagine a black shield that surrounds those things that we keep hidden. The first fight occurs when we feel as though someone is stepping behind that black shield. The force field is triggered, and this affects what we think, feel, say, and do next. We will do whatever is necessary to create space between us and the other person, because we have begun to feel that they are no longer safe for us.

Triggers and Landmines

Let's look again at my story of the anniversary trip. Though it wasn't our first fight, you can look at the argument Cindy and I had and see where the emotional barrier went up. I told you that Cindy has a history of navigational frustration, and she hates the memories associated with it. But I didn't tell you about my own emotional history. I have a few landmines of my own.

My childhood was pretty similar to *Leave It to Beaver*. (I was the Beaver.) My parents were married, and they each worked full-time. My dad's job covered the bills, and my mom's job paid for the extras. They made sure my sisters and I had quality educations and a strong work ethic (both of which we hated at the time but deeply appreciate now). My mother was always strong and assertive, one of the first in the women's lib movement. She modeled strength and decision-making in a culture where women were just learning to stretch that muscle. My father was more focused on our family than on his career, and he chose not to climb the corporate ladder because he wanted to invest his time and energy in us. You could set the clock by the time he pulled into the garage each evening. He was home for dinner every night, he was at all of my sports events, and he even watched most of the practices. My parents created a very solid home life for us, and I've always recalled my childhood as a happy one.

Looking back on it now, however, I can see how emotionally disconnected we were. My mom and dad loved my sisters and me very much, but they loved us imperfectly. There was a lot of tension in our home, usually centered around finances. Money was very important to my mother, and she never felt as though my dad earned enough. She would have been much more happily married to a man who was climbing the corporate ladder, but that's not who my dad was. My mom was the dominant one and the ultimate decision maker, and my dad was never strong enough to engage her as an equal and insist on equal decision-making. I don't ever remember seeing them address their issues in front of us, and I certainly never saw any conflict resolution.

They each had anger issues. I knew I was loved, but I didn't hear it very often. We just didn't talk about our emotions very much, so I didn't grow up with the tools to navigate emotions and relationships very well. My dad's anger came out with loud impatience. When I recall working on projects with him in the garage, I can see the cigarette hanging out of his mouth, one eye squinted shut as the smoke curled up into his eyes. If I misunderstood the directions, or if I didn't get a tool quickly enough for him, he would bark at me. Meanwhile, my mom stuffed her anger until it built up and leaked out in sarcastic comments. She was not touchy-feely, and I don't remember very many hugs or kisses. My sisters and I weren't close, and all three of us have wounds.

My mother was the life of the party, but she entertained the room with a biting, sarcastic wit. I was in seventh grade in the 1960s, and I had a very serious crush on the gorgeous redheaded girl who lived across the alley from us. I was deeply enamored with her. One summer day, while her mom and my mom were talking, the pretty girl and I were standing on the sidewalk with them. Out of the blue, my mom made a comment about the fluorescent green socks I was wearing. (It may be hard to imagine, but they were in fashion at the time.) This happened fifty years ago, and I can still recall the shame and embarrassment I felt over my mom pointing out my green socks. When something or someone makes me feel incompetent, I feel triggered. I get anxious, and I will respond. It won't be pretty. On that day, something broke within me, and I have since carried a wound attached to that emotional trigger.

What Is an Emotional Trigger?

We all have emotional triggers, so let's talk about these for a moment. An emotional trigger can be activated by a person, a situation, an event, a joke, a book, a commercial, a song on the radio, or even a scent in the air. These moments remind us of old, painful feelings, and they provoke a strong emotional response. Often, we are not aware when we are triggered; we simply seem to overreact in a big way to a small situation. That's why it's called a "trigger"—it is an automatic reaction that can be lightning fast.

You may become emotionally triggered when someone speaks sharply to you, ignores you or is too busy for you, or is trying to control you. You may become triggered if you are alone in an unfamiliar place, someone sneaks up behind you, your mate flips out the lights without warning, or you sense dishonesty in someone. Not all emotional triggers are negative, as we also have positive emotions that can be triggered just as easily. But for the purposes of this chapter, as we talk about the ways we hurt one another without meaning to, we will look at the effects of negative emotional triggers.

When Cindy didn't have the GPS up and running fast enough for me, I feared I would make a wrong turn and appear inept. That anxiety and insecurity triggered memories of my dad barking at me and my mom ridiculing my socks, and all of this caused me to be impatient with my wife. Without even realizing it, I revisited a time when someone had embarrassed me for doing the wrong thing, and Cindy was taken back to an environment where someone had dominated her and made all the decisions. We were each triggered by wounds from long before we ever met. Our black shields went up, and we reacted in ugly ways. It happens.

Just as the GPS in our cars determines where we should go next by identifying our position on the map, we each have our own internal GPS that guides our decisions based on where we *feel* we are in a current situation. It "locates us" when we are young and shapes our worldview, and this worldview guides the way we see all our relationships. It drives our responses to the people and situations around us. And just as a computer GPS needs an update as new roads and routes are added to the city grid, we can also benefit from some fine-tuning and redirection as we look at the changes in our path—where we've been, where we're going, what has gone wrong, and how we can do things differently. But if our actions are driven by our wounds instead of by intentional decisions, we can end up on the wrong path entirely. But when we are aware of our decisions, even if means taking the harder path, we can end up where we wanted to be all along.

The Decision in Every Fight

We hit emotional barriers again and again and again with one another. That's what marriage is about. The intensity may ebb and flow, but the nature of life together causes us to rub up against one another and trigger our emotional barriers. In every fight, beginning with the first one, you and your beloved are faced with a decision: "Are we willing to work though this? Or is this gap too far to cross? Am I willing to stay in this conversation, or is this too much to bear?"

I have discovered that when most people say, "I do," they're really saying, "I will stay with you as long as you make me happy." The more I do this work, the more I like the traditional wedding vows. The commitment really is for richer and for poorer, in sickness and in health, until death parts you. When each individual is committed to the marriage, then together they can figure out how to deal with the blessings and challenges that life throws at them.

In a marriage that is healthy and thriving, you continue to say to one another, "I'm in. It's difficult, but I'm in. This hurts a lot, but I'm staying in this." That's what it comes down to, again and again and again. We navigate the emotional barriers of life together by continuing to engage in ways that draw us close once again. In the moment when your beloved shoots up an emotional barrier to push you away, you are in charge of your response. And in that moment of conflict, nothing will be more important than how you communicate your love.

When we keep top-of-mind awareness that nothing is more important than conveying love to the other person, then we can work together to find answers to any issues that arise.

TOOL FOR THE JOURNEY:

No issue will ever be more important than how we communicate our love to one another.

Write this down and post it in a prominent place in your home. Choose to remember, on good days and bad days, that nothing will ever matter more than how well you are conveying love to one another.

Think about:

- Let yourself recall when you first became interested in your beloved.

- What drew you to this person?

- How did he or she look and act?

- What did you enjoy about his or her mind and worldview?

- What did you discover that you both enjoyed?

- What did you have in common?

- Did this chapter provoke any thoughts or memories of the ways your parents or other significant adults in your life have loved you and yet wounded you?

Talk about:

- Reminisce together about your first impressions of each other.

- Name specific details of those early memories that attracted you to each other.

- Share with your beloved any childhood memories you have of someone loving you yet wounding you.

CHAPTER THREE

"Ouch! Too Close!"

Welcome to the Wounded

WHEN OUR DAUGHTER ANNOUNCED to us that she was pregnant, our conversation turned quickly to what our names would be in this new role. There are a lot of parents and stepparents in our extended family, which made for a long list of grandparents, each of whom needed a new name. Cindy turned to me and said, "And what would you like to be called?"

Let me tell you this about my wife: Cindy couldn't wait to be a grandmother. She grew up right next door to her fun grandma, and the upstairs room was a space reserved especially for Cindy and her two sisters. She has wonderful memories of her grandmother, and she was eager to be one too. I, on the other hand, did not have such an upbringing. The only memory I have of my grandfather is a really sick old man who died when I was about five years old. I don't have good memories of him, and I didn't have any interest in becoming a grandparent. So, when she asked me what I'd like to be called, I said, "I think 'Grandpa Benish, sir' will be appropriate." (Okay, you can stop laughing now.)

But then our granddaughter was born, and you don't need me to tell you this, but I'll say it anyway: *everything changed.* Babies have a way of swooping into our lives and turning us inside out. On top of this consuming love for this newborn, we had an unexpected turn of events. My daughter's C-section incision became severely infected, and she was hospitalized for several weeks. With the new mom in recovery, I took care of our newborn granddaughter for the first month of her life. Though I had expected to be distant from my grandparenting role, my granddaughter, Trista, and I became quite attached to each other. And while I had teasingly thought I'd have her call me "Grandpa Benish, sir," I acquired a new name in those first few weeks: Grandpa Nanny. (To my great delight, the children still call me Grandpa Nanny. When we meet the kids for dinner at a restaurant, the two grandkids will come running across the parking lot, pumping their arms and yelling out to me, "Grandpa Nanny! Grandpa Nanny!" We get some odd looks from people standing by, but I wear that name with pride.)

We Are Born Selfish

I can tell you without a doubt that when I was Trista's full-time caregiver in that first month as Grandpa Nanny, she was the neediest, most selfish little being you can imagine. Not once did she fix a single meal for me. I fixed every bottle for her, I changed every single diaper, and she would hardly let me go to the bathroom. She was a little bundle of selfishness. That's because we all are. We are born that way.

I'm still that way. When I'm in traffic, I want all of those people in front of me to get out of my way, and I want all of the lights to stay green. I don't like to admit that I'm selfish, but the truth is, I am. I want what I want, when I want it, and I want it now. The Cookie Monster on *Sesame Street* is the G-rated version when he says, "See cookie! Want cookie! Me eat cookie!" The real-life version is, "See cookie! Want cookie! If you get between me and cookie, me going to get ugly!"

Thinking back to our anniversary trip, "the cookie" was my need to look competent, to know the right turns. I was completely irrational. Cindy and I didn't have any time restraints, we had nowhere we had to be, and it didn't make any difference how fast we got there. The excitement in the air was tangible, and I wouldn't have thought anything could ruin our perfect evening. Except that I ruined it because I'm selfish and needy. I was born that way, and so were you.

This inherent flaw in each of us is actually similar to the space command module in the movie I love, *Apollo 13*. The spacecraft had a flaw in it that stemmed from its manufacturing. The flaw was unknown; the engineers wouldn't have sent it into orbit knowing that it was imperfect. In the same way, we have flaws that we're not aware of, and they stem from our very beginnings. We are born selfish and flawed.

It Started in the Garden

Ultimately, mankind's brokenness started with Adam and Eve and the forbidden fruit. Before they ate of the fruit, there was total nakedness, and not just in the physical sense. They were fully known on every level—physically, emotionally, spiritually, and cognitively. God knew everything they did, thought, and felt. But when they each ate the apple, suddenly they became afraid to be seen. They covered themselves up because they were ashamed of their nakedness. They began playing hide-and-seek with a God whom they knew is all-knowing, which wasn't very intelligent, but that's the first evidence we have that we don't operate with great intelligence when we are wounded. Adam and Eve show the root of our tendency that says, "I don't want to reveal my ugly parts." But the reality is that we all have ugly parts because we all fall short of perfection.

As a result, God had to kick them out of the Garden of Eden. Up to then, they'd lived a very cushy life. Everything had been provided for, and though they labored in the Garden, it wasn't considered work. "Work" became a four-letter word after they got kicked out. And He didn't just boot them from the garden; he posted cherubim at the gate, and a flaming sword:

> After he drove the man out, he placed on the east side
> of the Garden of Eden cherubim and a flaming sword
> flashing back and forth to guard the way to the tree of
> life. (Genesis 3:24)

A cherub is not a Hallmark angel doll. It's a great big, fierce, scary creature. Since the verse uses the word "cherubim," the plural for *cherub*, we know there was more than one of those big, fierce, scary creatures. With cherubim standing at the entrance, and a sword flashing to and fro, there was no way back inside. When God banished Adam and Eve, they experienced abandonment. They could only go out into the wilderness, out into the great unknown. They had to do life on their own somehow, and they had to figure it out without the constant support of intimacy with God. (Obviously, they didn't do a very good job of it. Look how their kids turned out.) When sin entered the world, as you and I both know, everything changed. Creation was no longer perfect, and people became complicated, hurting beings with needs, wounds, brokenness, and selfishness.

As marriage partners, we need to admit that there are times when we treat our spouses as if they are the enemy. This awareness is where heart change can begin. Your partner is your beloved, the second-best gift God has given to you. But with all the intentional love in the world, each of you will still make damaging, hurtful mistakes in the ways you approach and treat one another. There is a reason for this, and it's a statement every single one of us has in common:

> **I am a wounded, needy, broken, selfish person,**
> **incapable of loving myself or anyone else perfectly.**
> **I am married to (or in a relationship with)**
> **a wounded, needy, broken, selfish person,**
> **incapable of loving themselves or anyone else perfectly.**

When we can return to this awareness and see objectively the ways we are driven by our brokenness— even when we don't mean to be, then we can begin to make changes in the right direction.

We Have to Pick a Word

Needy, wounded, broken, selfish. Those four words blend into and overlap each other in consuming ways that are deeper than our awareness. I've tried to blend them into one new word: *needy-wounded-broken-selfish*, but that's a mouthful. Just one of them doesn't seem like enough, and yet it's difficult to find a different word that succinctly sums up all of those words.

Wounded is pretty close to encompassing, but I don't know if we really see our need as a wound. Further, the word *wounded* certainly doesn't cover all of our selfishness, and we are all far more selfish than we want to admit. Still, it's too much to always say needy-wounded-broken-selfish, and *wounded* is as close as we have found so far. From here forward, when I'm talking about our neediness-woundedness-brokenness-selfishness, I'll use the word *wound* or *wounded* to describe the baggage we carry around. (But again, understand that the components that affect our behavior are bigger, deeper, wider, and more personal than one measly word implies.)

Our wounds drive our behavior, actions, thoughts, and feelings, and it starts in that very first month of our lives. We can't avoid it, we can't get around it, and we spend the rest of our lives trying to manage it. It's just how it goes and how it will be, this side of heaven.

I wish it were different. I know you do too.

TOOL FOR THE JOURNEY:

I am a wounded, needy, broken, selfish person,
incapable of loving myself or anyone else perfectly.
I am married to [or in a relationship with]
a wounded, needy, broken, selfish person,
incapable of loving himself or herself or anyone else
perfectly.

Think about:

- Can you think of a time when you treated your beloved as the enemy?

- How does it feel to admit that?

- In what ways are you selfish?

- How does this have a separating effect on your relationship?

Talk about:

Ask your beloved:

- "What am I doing right?"

- "How and when do you feel most loved by me?"

- "What do I do that makes you feel unloved? Unsafe?"

- "What are the things I do that make you want to pull away, rather than draw close?"

- "What have I done right in the past?"

- "When have I made you feel like you felt when we first fell in love?"

CHAPTER FOUR

The Fears That Drive Us
Abandonment and Intimacy

WHAT WAS RATIONAL ABOUT my behavior in the car with Cindy the night we intended to celebrate our anniversary—then didn't? Nothing. I was impatient and gruff with her. A rational husband would have taken a few minutes to let the GPS boot up, but I wasn't in a rational place. I love Cindy, adore her, and I want her to become all that she can become, so why don't I treat her that way? If I were a rational being, it would make sense that I would treat her with flawless affection and priority. And yet, often, I become part of the problem, and I trigger her wounds.

Are you a rational being?

It's one of my favorite questions in my marriage workshops, because we live in a culture that is deeply focused on rationality. We think we are logical, rational people. But I am on a mission to get people to disavow that notion. We are not rational beings. Our behaviors are often irrational. We are driven by unconscious forces; hence, we are *ir*rational beings.

We don't like that notion, because we like to think we are in charge of ourselves, but let me ask you what may seem to be a random question: what is the sole purpose of perfume? It is a largely unconscious force that's supposed to attract our behavior. I'm attracted to some perfumes, and I am repulsed by others. Research shows that pheromones also affect what we are attracted to: it is all subconscious. We are driven by forces that we have very little conscious knowledge of.

So, what are the forces that drive you? Part of learning to love intentionally means you must shine a flashlight into the cobwebs of your story, and your partner's. You can then begin to identify what motivations are hiding deep in there, and you can bring them into the light. Once you name it, your can navigate it, rather than letting it control you.

Two Fears That Drive Us

Emotionally speaking, we each have one thing we believe we need in order to survive. We tend to fight for either: (1) security and commitment, or (2) privacy and space. It may seem overly simplistic, but this is ultimately what drives our behaviors. We want to feel safe, but a sense of safety feels different for each person. Either we want to be seen and known, or we want to protect ourselves from being seen and known. The greatest turmoil exists when the two collide: we want companionship, but we are terrified of someone coming too close. We all have one of these primary fears, and some of us have both of them. But I haven't yet seen anybody who didn't have one or the other.

A person with a *fear of abandonment* is one who values security above all else. He wants his partner to stay close, both physically and emotionally. He needs words of assurance, calming hugs of commitment, and for his partner to be available in every way. For this person, safety involves moving closer to the other person. This fear of abandonment tends to stem from a past experience of being abandoned, or with the perception of being abandoned. Whenever a person with an abandonment issue *perceives* emotional distance from the other person, he will react, usually by pursuing the other person. He will want to cling tightly, hold on, grasp, pursue, and control.

A person with a *fear of intimacy* is one who values space above all else. She needs emotional space, and she doesn't like to feel pursued too intensely. She does need words of affirmation and patience from her beloved, and she thrives with someone who is a pillar of emotional acceptance. But clinging and grasping cause her to step back. Her fear of intimacy tends to stem from an experience of sharing intimacy with someone who responded poorly. This may have been a parent who was emotionally absent, so as a child, she felt that she had nobody safe to confide in. It may have taken root in a household that was emotionally disconnected, where lots of things were going wrong that nobody was talking about. Or the fear may have come from someone learning a secret and betraying a sacred trust. Someone with a fear of intimacy has decided, either consciously or subconsciously, that she won't let anyone get too close. If she keeps walls up, others may never know her well enough to hurt her. And if she perceives that someone is getting too close, then she will either pull away or push away—whatever she must do to create separation. She's got to create distance with a solid emotional barrier.

Adam and Eve showed us the beginning of these two major fears we carry into relationships: the fear of intimacy, and the fear of abandonment. When they ate the apple and then hid from God, the fear of intimacy was born, because they didn't want to be seen too closely. When they were banished from the garden and could never return to their safest place, the fear of abandonment was born, because they felt abandoned and alone.

Our fears make us believe we must have the thing we crave. We become motivated to protect that which we think we cannot live without, whether it is someone coming too close or getting too far away. Fears block us from our best decisions and behaviors, limiting the potential for individuals and for relationships. We cannot let our fear of what might happen block the greater good. Fear destroys relationships.

Emotions on Display

Can we accept that none of us is perfect? If we can agree with that basic assumption, then we can agree with and accept that our parents weren't perfect either. My parents loved and provided for me and my two sisters to the very best of their abilities, but their love was still imperfect. With imperfect parents, we each develop wounds and fears of intimacy or abandonment. A lot of people confuse the two fears. It's true that the behaviors each fear causes can look similar, but the *root cause* is different.

Most of our lives are made up of our responses to the behavior and emotions on display around us. Moments unfold around us all day long, and each one triggers a response that you may or may not notice. Some moments make you smile, like when your dog wags her tail when you wake up in the morning. Or when an oldies song plays on the radio, and you remember your freshman year in college, when that song was in the Top 40.

Other moments bring frustration. Your kid sleeps through the alarm, even though it's buzzing loud enough to wake everyone in the neighborhood. You get stuck behind a garbage truck on your way to work, and now you'll be a few minutes late to your first appointment. You get a notice that the library books are overdue *again*.

Still, other moments make you downright angry. Your wife comments that you're acting "just like your father." You discover that your checking account is overdrafted because your spouse ignored the budget. Your children are arguing *again* over whose night it is to do the dishes. Some things are just too much, and they push you to the very edge.

We spend our days navigating these ups and downs, and while some of them never make it onto our radar, others seem to ruffle our feathers and raise our blood pressure. You probably know what kinds of things usually make you angry, and you likely know how you tend to respond. But what causes that response, really? It may feel it's out of your control, that it's just how you're wired. You may not have an awareness of your triggers. You may feel that the problem is the dishes overflowing in the sink, or the driving habits around you in your morning commute, but it is perhaps deeper. And it's possible to know what lies underneath it all, what is hiding in there and giving energy to that reaction.

This awareness calls for some humility, and—let's just say it—sometimes humility is painful. But this is truly the first step toward change in the heart of your marriage or relationship.

Perception and Understanding

Perception is a big part of reality. If four people witness a car accident, you'll get four different accounts of the same accident. We all perceive the world and our lives through our own fractured lenses, and those lenses have been fractured by our wounds. What you experience may be true, but it is not necessarily accurate. How you feel cannot be denied, but it may not accurately reflect the facts of what actually happened.

This past weekend, Cindy and I hosted a dinner party with two other couples: my collaborative writer and her husband, and my publisher and his wife. We had a lovely time of sharing stories and catching up over dinner (and the French onion soup was outstanding, if I do say so myself). As I listened to the group conversation, I noticed a pattern among all three of us couples: we tended to tell stories the same way. My wife invited me to tell the story of how we came to buy our house, but I didn't get very far into the story before she had to jump in and add a detail she felt I had forgotten or overlooked. Sometimes I would invite Cindy to tell a story, and then I would jump in to "correct" her version of the story. Both of the other couples did the very same thing! It's an example of how perception affects our understanding. Each of the couples had experienced their memories together, but they had lived through their stories in very different ways. Different details emerged as more or less important, depending on who was telling the story.

One of the most challenging aspects in working with couples is the differences in perception. A husband and wife will come to me, and one of them will make statements about what he or she believes to be the problem. Those statements usually sound like, "I know the truth." Well, no, you don't know. It is your *perception* of what has happened or what was said. It may surprise you to learn that it's possible for someone to physically hear something that's very different from the words that were spoken. It happens quite frequently, actually, and Cindy and I are not exempt from this. We can have conversations where she'll say, "These are the words I used," but those are definitely not the words I heard. We can spin all day long in a debate about who is right and who is wrong, but then we are stuck in the weeds. We won't go anywhere. We'll only damage our relationship. I see it all the time in my counseling office. One person will say, "You just said this and this . . ." and I'll have to interrupt to say, "No, that's not what he said. What he said was . . ." Our minds can deceive us based on our perception.

This can also happen with wounds from your childhood. You may feel as though your dad abandoned you, perhaps in a divorce situation, but it could be that the mom was being obstructive and wouldn't let your dad see you. There may have been no way for you to know what was really happening, and you have grown up with feelings based on your perceptions. Perception changes the meaning entirely, and that is the reality we have to deal with.

Perception is not about right and wrong, or more specifically, *who is right* and *who is wrong*. You have your perception that is valid, and the other person has a perception that is also valid. I must accept Cindy's perceptions of life in general, especially as her life pertains to me, and she must accept mine as well. Perception is not a question of either/or, but rather a matter of both/and. The question is not whether Cindy is right or whether I am, but instead, it is *both* Cindy *and* I who have our very own—very real—perceptions. Each of us needs to engage the other's perception.

Knowing Yourself

The truth is, you are a wounded, broken, needy, and selfish person, driven by a fear you may not be able to name, and you are married to someone of whom this is also true. You are incapable of loving yourself or the other person perfectly, and yet no issue between you should ever be more important than how you convey your love to each other. These core truths live in tension with one another, as they are polarizingly opposite but also abundantly true.

The question, then, is, how do we mesh multiple perceptions together to make decisions that help us deal with this life together? Well, we need to look at each of our wounds and the fears that drive us. When we begin to explore these together, we also begin to understand how those wounds and fears have impacted the way we see the world, how we perceive events that happen to us, and how we often relate to the people we love most. These discoveries can lead to "light bulb" moments of crystal clarity.

TOOL FOR THE JOURNEY:

Our behaviors are driven by a fear that other people will get too close, or that they will abandon us. When we can identify our basic fear, of intimacy or of abandonment, we can begin to learn why we do the things we do—to others and to ourselves.

Think about:

- Do you already have a sense of which fear is greater in you?

- It is usually easier to see fears in someone else before you can identify your own. Consider other people in your life. Can you identify which fear is greater is their lives?

- Are you the one who pursues your beloved to deal with issues, or are you the one who avoids dealing with the issues?

- What makes you angry? Why do you think this causes a reaction in you?

- When someone gets in your face, do you engage or escape?

- How do you feel when the other person walks away or shuts down when you are trying to discuss an issue?

- Consider your childhood. Were your parents emotionally available and connected with you? (I never want to demonize or put blame on parents. In the majority of cases, they loved their children to the best of their ability, but they still loved imperfectly.)

  o Think of a crisis or calamity that occurred during your elementary or middle school years. This may be a sickness, a surgery, a injury, or a legal issue. How did your parents respond?

  o Were you able to confide in either of your parents, both of them, or neither of them? How did you feel about them?

- Think about other significant relationships throughout your life.

  o Have you struggled to share your feelings and innermost thoughts?

  o Did you tend to hang on to relationships, even though they weren't healthy, after it was pretty clear the relationships were over, or after others encouraged you to end them?

o   Think about your last failed relationship. Were you the one to end it, or was the other person?

o   Do you see yourself as the one in control or the one being controlled?

Talk about:

- Listen to your beloved tell a story that you were part of. (It doesn't have to be a controversial story or the recall of a fight between you. In fact, it's better to start with a funny or interesting story that involved both of you.) As he or she tell it, think of how your perspective is different. When he or she finishes, share your perspective. Then, reverse roles. Tell a story while your partner listens and writes down his or her different perspective.

    o   Remember: There is typically not a *right* perspective and a *wrong* perspective. There can be more than one perspective. Each person's job is to listen, receive, and accept, but he or she does not have to agree. You can accept the other person's perspective as his or her truth, though your truth may look and sound very different.

- Discuss the process you went through from the "Think About section" and share what you think is your greater fear and why. Ask your partner for his or her thoughts and observations.

- Together, share ideas for how you could interact with each other in ways that would be helpful and connecting.

- Share with one another things that trigger your fears. It could be a tone of voice, a mannerism, specific words, or body language.

- Agree on one or two ways each of you is willing to be held accountable to change how you interact with the other.

CHAPTER FIVE

The Beautiful Possibilities in Pain
The Relational Model

LET'S GO BACK TO those early stages of your relationship, the glorious few weeks or months before that first fight. Earlier, we talked about our behavioral connection with someone new, then the cognitive connection, and finally, the emotional connection—these all unfold before we hit that first emotional barrier. I believe that while we think we are attracted to another person because of the way he or she looks and thinks, and because we like so many of the same things, God is at work on a much deeper level. I am more and more convinced that He is at work in that wounded place in each of us. He has allowed you to become attracted to—and attractive to—someone whose brokenness will trigger yours, and your brokenness will trigger his or hers. You see, when we trigger each other's wounds, we create conflict in our relationship. These conflicts are unpleasant, but they ultimately bring our wounds into the light so they may be healed.

(And you thought that first date was just about a cup of coffee.)

Layers of Protection

Do you remember taking earth science class, probably in about seventh grade, when our teachers taught us about the earth's structure and how its go deeper and deeper, from the rocky crust to the fiery core? I think that's a fairly adequate description of our emotional patterns. Each of us is made up of many emotional layers that we have to work through as we get to know each other more deeply, and all of these layers are hiding what's near our core: our woundedness, brokenness, neediness, and selfishness. These can be what we are most ashamed of, and we work very diligently—both consciously and subconsciously—to keep these fiery secrets hidden from our partners, from God, and even from ourselves. We hide behind a spiritual barrier that is a lot like Adam's and Eve's fig leaves (see Genesis 3:7). They would do anything to keep from being exposed, and we are the same way.

The emotional barrier and the spiritual barrier are similar in that they both have the same job: to protect us. However, they protect us from different things. The emotional barrier protects me from other people and from my conscious self, and the spiritual barrier is the way I hide from God. On a cognitive level, I can understand that God knows everything about me, but in my experience, I don't really want to reveal that to Him. Just as I cannot reveal all of my wounds to another person without a filter in between us, I also want that kind of space between me and God as I work through the process of letting Him in. It's a process, as we begin to reveal ourselves.

Conflict Is Not a Bad Thing

We are drawn, unknowingly or unconsciously, to people who will trigger and expose our wounds, and we will trigger and expose their wounds. That causes a conflict, and for you, one of two things can happen:

> your interaction with them can either bring healing to their wounds, their souls, and their lives; or

> your interaction can make everything worse by slicing and dicing their hearts and souls.

Pain isn't something you're supposed to *avoid* when you're in relationship; it's actually what you're supposed to *lean into,* as this is the path to healing, delighting, being vulnerable, and loving one another more deeply. Instead of avoiding your beloved's hurting heart, you can show your partner that you see and know him or her, and you can bring healing to his or her heart by loving your partner well.

The world handles conflict very differently from how God wants us to. When we approach conflict, we are motivated by confrontation and the need to win. (We are also motivated by a desire to control, punish, and protect ourselves, and all of these motivations stem from a desire to win the battle.) If we follow the world's model, conflict almost always leads to emotional separation, and we react to the other person's outward behavior, words, thoughts, and feelings with our own unlovable behavior. This unlovable behavior can play out in any number of ways: name calling, withholding sex, withdrawing, yelling, and hitting below the belt. When your partner behaves in unlovable ways, you tend to respond in ways that are equally unlovable.

It's so hard to ignore hurtful behavior, isn't it? When it feels like arrows shot at your heart, salt poured into your cut, and hot tar poured on your soul, it's so hard to stay vulnerable and choose not to take a defensive, self-protective stance. But it is possible to take a step back, watch what's going on, and begin to see what's giving energy to this unlovable behavior. Usually the behavior is hiding a sentiment such as, "I'm afraid," or "I don't feel safe." When you can see past the behavior and into the wound, you can learn to love at a very deep level.

When we handle conflict the way God has designed, we choose a different path from the world's. Instead of creating distance, we seek to have eyes to see and ears to hear the woundedness that is driving those behaviors, thoughts, and words. When your partner does something unlovable, you can choose to take it not quite so personally, to see that it's not about you at all, and to seek to understand which of your own wounds are being triggered. You can ignore behavior that offends you, and instead you can recognize that it's only a symptom of a deeper wound, either within the person you love or yourself. When you can see the wound that's really driving unpleasant behavior, then you can become an agent to help heal or manage that wounds.

Here is the most beautiful part of this process: it begins to feed itself. When you respond at a deeper level of love instead of fueling the flame of conflict, your spouse will begin to feel safer, known, and willing to go deeper as well. This builds a greater sense of safety and trust, which tightens the bonds of relationship and draws you closer to one another, which creates an even greater sense of safety and trust . . . and the cycle goes on and on.

A Healing Tool in Marriage

I believe that this journey in life—the process of learning how to have healthier relationships, how to love myself, and how to love others better—is centered around the notion of understanding my behaviors, what drives them, and what gives them energy. My behaviors are driven by my wounded sense of who I am, and I need safe people to help me break down those barriers that I keep around my wounded self.

When I have been intentional about learning my partner's history and the actions or words that trigger a negative response in her, I have loved her better. As I continue to discover these things, I can create a space that feels safe for her because I am more aware of my own wounds and triggers. We need to become aware of our own landmines—even as we become aware of our partners'—so we can avoid placing blame and pointing fingers. It's tempting to say that an angry environment at home, in a relationship, or in a marriage is someone else's fault, but there are always two sides to an interaction. If your partner triggers a response in you, it's healthy and important to figure out what part of your story may be the true cause of that pain, rather than jump to blaming the other person for causing this uncomfortable or painful response.

The art of healing is one Jesus knew and modeled so well, and that healing can happen on so many levels. God can heal us, and we can heal one another. With light in our dark places, we become more and more aware of our wounds and triggers. As Cindy's spouse, I can poke holes in her emotional barriers to let the light and healing in. She can do the same for me. When I allow God to be at the core of who I am, and when I allow him to drive my conscious behavior, feelings, and thoughts, then

I am able to treat Cindy as the gift God has given to me.

This can be revolutionary.

TOOL FOR THE JOURNEY:

Conflict is not a bad thing when intentional interaction can bring healing to the wounds of the past. There can be beautiful possibilities in pain.

Think about:

- Recall an argument you had with your beloved, when you pulled away.

- Ask yourself: What part of my story or my past caused me to react this way?

- Ask yourself: What would happen if I chose not to pull away? What would it look like if I leaned into the hurt instead, to see what hurt is hiding behind this behavior?

- Keep a list of the answers you come up with. Share these with your partner.

Talk about:

- Recall together a time when the two of you had a spat that caused one or both of you to pull away.

- Ask your partner: "Did I say or do something on that day that caused you to pull away?"

- Ask your partner: "How can I be more engaging and less confrontational?"

- Any time you sense distance or a defensive tone in a conversation with your partner, stop and say, "I sense something has changed. I want to learn how to do this better and how to love you better. What did I do just now that caused you to take a step back from me?"

- Keep a list of your partner's answers. Also keep track of what you learn about the patterns in your conversations and what causes confrontation between the two of you.

PART TWO

What Is Intentional Love?

Five Ways to Love Better Sooner

WE LIVE IN A "Just do it" society. Want a new car? Just do it. Struggling in your marriage and thinking about finding a new partner? Just do it. Finances a little tight? Just refinance the mortgage and pull out your equity. Or simply get another credit card. Just do it.

Just do it. Just do it. *Just do it.*

The problem is, this way often leads to bondage. The new car is old and in need of repairs long before the monthly payments are finished. The divorce rate for second marriages is more than 50 percent higher than for first marriages, and the rate for third marriages is 80 percent higher. In fact, some studies have shown that a large percentage of men—and an even larger percentage of women—are as angry or angrier ten years after their divorce as they were at the time of their divorce. When it comes to finances, the average household has credit card debt, auto loans, mortgage debt, and student loans, and mounting lists of other miscellaneous debt. We are drowning in our bad decisions. Time doesn't erase the bad feelings that go untended, and debts don't pay themselves. Hope is not a strategy.

But there is another way, a disciplined journey that leads to freedom rather than bondage. You can choose the path of trust by practicing intentional love. Realizing that we are irrational beings can make us feel a little bit out of control. But we have the power to make a choice: Do I want to live in fear, or do I want to practice love? Do I want my life to be driven by wounds, or do I want my life to be based on trust?

Cindy and I have a strong marriage that has survived many challenges, weathered many storms, and welcomed many celebrations. I will admit, after our two decades, we do not have the pizazz of our early days, but what we have instead is a depth and breadth we didn't have when we began this love story. We have a foundation that fosters peace, contentment, and joy that just weren't possible in the fireworks of the earliest days. How did we get here? By choosing again and again and again to trust each other, and by being intentional about making each other feel loved.

In part 2 I'd like to share with you the model that we've claimed for our marriage, and it's one that I teach to couples all over the country. It involves the five practices involved in the art of intentional love: sacrifice, delight, healing, vulnerability, and forgiveness. Let's dive into these five practices as a way to create the pegboard I described in the opening pages. These are the "hooks" where you can hang your tools.

CHAPTER SIX

The Art of Service and Sacrifice
The Best Part of Waking Up

CINDY AND I LIKE to start our day with a cup of coffee in bed. I'm a morning person, and my wife is not. (She's not a night person, either. She prefers to call herself a middle-of-the-day person.) I tend to wake up earlier, and even if we're waking up together to an alarm, I still move faster than she does. Ninety percent of the time, I'm the one who gets up, brews the coffee, pours it into two mugs, and bring them to our bed.

I am happy to do this for my wife, and I do this without any angst or resentment. There is no feeling put-upon. It is not a burden, and I don't say, "Here, sweetie. Let me bring you a cup of coffee in bed—*again.*" I'm happy to do this for her because I know that I'm a morning person. Now, on the rare occasion when she is up before me, when she brews the coffee and brings my mug to me in bed, I can tell you those mornings are especially sweet—and I'm not referring just to the flavor of the coffee. Even though she doesn't make it quite the same way I do, it's exceptionally delicious because she served me. It's something we do for each other, and we are very intentional about thanking the other one for serving.

Jesus modeled the art of serving throughout His ministry on earth, in the big and small ways He interacted with the people around Him. His first miracle happened at the wedding where He turned water into wine. Hospitality was a great value in that culture, and the shame of running out of wine would have affected the family's standing forever in their community. Jesus could fix this, and by serving them, He changed their whole world.

The art of service and sacrifice unfolds in the big and small ways that you can change another person's moment or his or her whole world. By using your gifts and willingness to serve, you can bring about change. For example, when I choose to serve my wife by pouring a steamy mug of coffee for her, I can change the first moments of her morning, which can change the direction of her day, which can change the trajectory of our marriage.

In a healthy relationship, both people are willing to set aside their own needs and preferences when they have an opportunity to serve each other. We don't serve because we have to, but rather because we *get* to. When you serve the other, you enable and empower that person to become who he or she was meant to be. (I am hesitant to use the word "enable" in this context, since it carries negative connotations of codependency. That's not the kind of enabling I'm referring to, but rather the lifting up and empowering that comes with knowing someone and loving him or her well.)

It's amazing what a morning cup can do, how it can set us on the right foot to start the day. Sure, the caffeine doesn't hurt, but more importantly, my wife and I start the day by serving one another. That's the best part of waking up.

Sacrifice Is Different

When we are talking about sacrifice, we go at least a little deeper than we do with service. There is a real cost involved, whether it is physical, emotional, or spiritual.

When Apollo 13 was preparing to launch, one of the astronaut—Ken Mattingly—got bumped from the crew because he had been exposed to the measles. NASA was pretty sure he was going to get very ill soon, so they put another astronaut in the spacecraft in his place. (Can you imagine that kind of devastation for Mattingly? He was two days away from a launch to the moon, so close to the actual culmination of his career, and he lost his spot on the crew over the *measles*.) When the explosion happened and they couldn't get the astronauts home, the engineers brought Mattingly into the simulator to figure out how to power up the reentry module. They had very tight power constrictions on the spacecraft, so they had shut down everything to conserve energy for as long as possible. Now that it was time to power everything up again, they had to do it in a very specific order. They couldn't exceed the power on the shuttle, and there just wasn't enough to go around. The team had been at it for twenty-four hours, and when yet another hypothesis failed, everyone was frustrated.

Mattingly said, "I have another idea. Let's try this again."

The guys on the control board said, "Are you sure you don't want to take a break?"

Mattingly said something like, "My buddies up there in the space capsule aren't getting a break. I'm not taking a break until we solve this." That is sacrifice.

How does this parallel with marriage? Well, when we choose to stay in a heated conversation until it cools down, when we stay in the relationship though it would be easier to walk away, when we can agree that nothing we want as individuals can be more important than our relationship with our spouse, then we make personal sacrifice for the benefit of the team: Team Us.

We also see sacrifice with sports teams, as individual players make personal sacrifices for the sake of the whole team. As I'm writing this book, the Philadelphia Eagles have just won Super Bowl 52, and the United States finished the 2018 Winter Olympics with twenty-three medals, including nine golds. Long before we get to watch the individuals and the teams compete, they have each spent countless hours in the gym, putting in the time to train. This is sacrifice. Let's see if I can give you a few examples of what this looks like in a marriage. Specifically, in my own.

A Move to a New Time Zone

When Cindy and I got the call for me to go to seminary, we both had the vision. We knew we needed to go. God had made it clear to us, so we turned our whole lives upside down by moving from California to Denver, and this move required huge sacrifices—especially on Cindy's part. You see, one of Cindy's great gifts is hospitality. She is an artist of interior design, and our home is her canvas. We had modified our California home exactly the way we loved it. We had one bathroom left to go before the house would be completely customized to our liking. We had redesigned the floor plan from a four-bedroom to a three-bedroom with a big master suite. We had taken out walls, moved them around, put in skylights, and spent a small fortune on the kitchen. Cindy had designed a Mediterranean patio out front, and we had built it ourselves. I learned how to build the walls, she learned how to stucco, and we poured a cement patio, tiled it, and put a fountain in the middle. In the backyard, we had a multitiered pond system that was surrounded by a flagstone patio. She had expanded her gardening, and we had tons of flowers. It was absolutely gorgeous inside and out. It was our sanctuary. And we would have to leave it behind.

Not only would we have to leave our sanctuary behind, but we'd also need to leave twenty-five years' worth of friends and acquaintances. Cindy's bosses at her job graciously offered to transfer her position and allowed her to work from home, but the idea of a home office was one thing in a town where we had lived for more than two decades with a vast social network. In Colorado, the only people we knew were my daughter and my son-in-law. She would have to rebuild not only her home and garden, but her whole social network, all while I would be up to my eyeballs in graduate school. The sacrifice was *huge*.

As I said, when we're talking about sacrifice, there is a very real cost involved. It may be physical, emotional, or spiritual. Cindy said yes to the move into a new time zone, knowing only a glimpse of what it would cost her. We moved to Denver, and we started over in every way. When we bought our Colorado home, one of the major selling points were the tons of raised flower beds already in place all over the property. I knew I needed to help get Cindy back into gardening, to get her hands back into the soil. In February in California, she was carrying in bushels of calla lilies from her garden and giving bouquets away to all our friends. In February in Colorado, all I could promise her were bushels of snow. So, when we found this house, it sang to her. Those flower beds spoke her love language.

The grounds of the new property had not been kept up for a long, long time. The beds had to be completely denuded, rejuvenated, and turned over. Now came my chance to make a small sacrifice in the wake of her bigger one: I can do the heavy work she isn't capable of doing. I turn the soil, I add the amendments, I rototill it, and I get the ground soft and ready. Then I walk away, and it's all ready for her to work her magic with those green thumbs. This is a sacrifice I can make of my time and energy.

If I'm honest, it's still not sacrificing, really. Sure, I wouldn't be doing it if she didn't need me to. And there is a cost in terms of my time and energy, though I do not dislike doing those things when I have the time and energy. But I like that I'm serving her with my hands. I can choose whether or not to do this for Cindy, and the choice isn't difficult. When we are each making a sacrifice for the other with our hearts in the right place, then we mutually fuel the desire to continue to serve one another. It's not a struggle.

TOOL FOR THE JOURNEY:

**The art of service and sacrifice unfolds
in the big and small ways
that I can change another person's moment
or his or her whole world.
By using my gifts and willingness to serve,
I can bring about change.**

Think about:

- Over the last week, how have you served your beloved? What sacrifices have you made? Make a list.

- Strive to make a complete list of all the ways your beloved has served you in the last week. (Make sure not to leave out the many tasks that are easily taken for granted!)

Talk about:

- At the end of the week, find a quiet space together. Share your list and your gratitude with your beloved.

CHAPTER SEVEN

The Art of Delight
From the Candlestick to the Flame

WHEN MOST PEOPLE TALK about love, they picture and describe something akin to the fireworks over Cinderella's castle at Disney World. Certainly, passion is part of love, but there's something much deeper to it. A whole lot more. With all the millions of words in our language, we are somehow still limited when it's time to find the ones we need.

The Eskimos have twenty-eight words for snow, and we have only one. The Hebrews have three words for love, and we only have one. How can there be so many words and yet so few to define what matters to us? It's especially difficult to define *love*. We need a couple hundred more to somehow explain what it is that lives and grows between us. It's so central to who we are and how we relate to one another, and we talk so much about it—we write poems and sonnets and songs about it. But nobody really knows how to define it.

Delight is a wonderful word. To delight means to please someone greatly, to bring that person great pleasure. It's a strong feeling of happiness or joy. When a person falls in love with his or her beloved, that individual feels enough delight to send him or her into orbit around the moon. Sadly, most of the couples I deal with have lost their delight, and they have forgotten that delight isn't just something you feel. It's something you can work on, and it is something you can choose.

A Picture of Delight

Delight has three layers: respect, honor, and cherish. Each is important, and they matter in that specific order. If you don't feel honored, then you cannot feel cherished; and if you don't feel respected, then you can't feel either honored or cherished. They build on one another.

Picture a wax candle in a brass candlestick. The brass candlestick is at the base, creating the foundation. The candlestick does not change shape, it will not change size, and it cannot change its consistency. The brass is solid, unchangeable, and foundational. In an analogy of delight, the brass candlestick represents respect. It is the foundation to everything else.

Next, the wax candle is on top of the candlestick, and it represents honor. You can put a different candle in the holder, with different colors or different fragrances.

Similarly, you can choose to honor your spouse in a myriad of ways throughout your day, week, years, and lifetime together. Honor looks different in various seasons, but it is an essential piece of delight.

Lastly, on the top is the flame of "cherish." It comes and goes, from stretching tall to flickering out. But it is built on the foundation of the other two. When you establish a foundation of respect, when you choose to honor, then you can light your spouse's fire with the flame of feeling cherished. You can make it your mission to never let that flame go out.

To Delight in Her Children

When Cindy and I began blending our families twenty years ago, her children, Andrew and Lara, were twelve and eight respectively, and my daughter, Tonya, was twelve. We had partial custody of Tonya, and we were headquarters for Andrew and Lara. Their dad lived a mile away from us, and they could visit him anytime they wanted, but they were with us most of the time. We were a family in a blender with three kids at crucial ages and important stages.

Cindy and I hit some bumps in the road, which I have come to understand are pretty classic and common when people are learning to parent together. You see, there is a spectrum of discipline styles. On one end is strong discipline, and on the other end is lenient discipline. What frequently happens, and what happened in our case, is that one of the adults is a strong disciplinarian, and the other is more liberal and lenient. In our case, I was the one pushing for discipline that was too rigid, while I felt that Cindy was overcompensating by pampering the kids. This became the number one struggle that Cindy and I had to work through, and it came to a head in the second or third year of our marriage. Both of us were frustrated, and neither of us could hear any message from the other on this topic. Cindy felt she had to defend the children from me, and I felt she was spoiling them.

Sometime in Andrew's middle school years, he decided he wanted to play the guitar. I could relate to that desire; when I was thirteen, I wanted the same thing. The reality is, I had *zero* musical skill. In fact, my middle school choir director had done everything she could to get me on pitch, including placing me between the two strongest singers. Sadly, they couldn't bring me to the right note. I only dragged them down with me. My ability to hear pitch was so very absent that the director finally gave me permission—or perhaps *instruction*—to simply mouth the words at the Christmas pageant. I was the only kid in the choir who was explicitly asked *not to sing*. And I was no better at the guitar.

I think it's a good thing for parents to encourage the interests and passions their children have, but parents also have an obligation to be wise about the path on which they place their children. Moms and dads should seek to understand what their children's gifts are, and then align the family decisions with those natural skills and abilities. Sure, I had asked for a guitar for Christmas, but I am confident that if they had chosen not to get it for me, I would have promptly forgotten about that fleeting whim. I would have moved on to something else. My Christmas list wasn't written in stone as my life's aspirations. But they got me the guitar, and they signed me up for lessons—a purchase and commitment that would cost a sacrificial amount of money for our family. I hated it all. I hated practicing for thirty minutes a day. I hated taking lessons. I hated the whole experience.

Fast-forward thirty years. The tables had turned, and history repeated itself. When we got Andrew his guitar, I did what my parents did: we also introduced him to weekly lessons, daily practicing, and heaps of self-discipline. After all, as my parents had so effectively taught me, the best way to learn to play an instrument is to take lessons and practice for a minimum of thirty minutes a day. I placed upon Andrew the responsibility of proving the guitar's worth. The guitar battles exhausted us all, until eventually Andrew stopped playing. It was a disaster that severely affected our relationship.

Thankfully, we found a counselor who helped us work through this gap in our approach. (Even professionals need help from time to time.) Here's what I learned: if I wanted to love Cindy well, then I needed to learn to love the flesh of her flesh. I wish I had learned to love better sooner, but it took me a few years to learn how to parent Andrew well. By the time Andrew was sixteen or seventeen, I had a lot of repairs to make. I had misunderstood him for a lot of years. Andrew went to Penn State when he graduated from high school. In part, he went to be closer to his dad's clan based in the East, but I also know that he wanted to escape from living with me. Lara was four years younger than him, so I still had some time to make some repairs before she left our home. I worked hard at loving her well.

In the guitar battles with Andrew, I failed to recognize that he is truly very talented musically. Andrew has wonderful hands to play the guitar, and he has the ear of a musician. Many years later, he taught himself how to play the guitar, and to this day, he has a garage band and they occasionally play gigs around town. Why couldn't I just let him play the guitar in the way that delighted him? He's really quite gifted in ways I surely am not. As I've said before, there are a few moments, decisions, conversations, and seasons of my life where I wish I could get a do-over. This is one of those. One of my regrets in my life is that I did not recognize, accept, and encourage Andrew's natural abilities. I think that's part of what it means to love someone: to discover that stuff. I dropped the ball and I missed my chance for a lot of years.

In the years to follow, I've become more and more aware of my mistakes in parenting a son. I have continued to focus on the repairs, taking ownership of what I did wrong. When Andrew got married a few years ago, Cindy and I decided that we would give him and his bride the gift of remodeling the master bathroom in their home. Their house was built in the 1920s, and it's a very cute house that needed a lot of work. Cindy suggested that I do the demolition and she do the building. I flew out to Pennsylvania, expecting that this would be a three-day job at the most. But once we got started, we discovered that the walls were four-inch thick plaster with chicken wire embedded in it. We had to use a circular saw to cut twelve-inch blocks out of the wall, and we had to carry each thirty-five-pound block downstairs and outside. We had masks over our faces, goggles over our eyes, and plastic over the doorways because the plaster was *everywhere*. The demolition took an entire week of twelve- to fourteen-hour days, and we coughed and sputtered our way through the whole thing. But do you know what? There was never a cross word between us. *That's* how far we've come.

What a gift to enjoy the fruit of our relationship! After a few years of some difficult mistakes, I learned how to love Andrew better, not just sooner. We changed our direction before it was too late. And my delight in her son was a gift to Cindy. To love him well was to love her well.

The Promise of the Sewing Machine

If you're not a quilter, you may not recognize the importance of a long-arm sewing machine. It's absolutely critical if you're going to do any actual quilting, which is where you take the top layer, the middle layer, and the backing, and you complete a sewing design to hold the batting in place so the whole quilt doesn't become all saggy and lumpy. The quilting step is a huge part of the creative process, and most quilting hobbyists send out to have that stage completed because they don't have the equipment in their homes.

There's a reason why most people don't have this machine: it costs a small *fortune*. You could probably get a long-arm machine for a couple thousand dollars, but a decent one costs between five thousand and twenty thousand dollars for a fully computerized machine equipped to finish a king-size quilt. They're not cheap; the investment is sizable. Cindy is an expert quilter, and a few years ago, it became clear to both of us that she had outgrown our equipment. She continued to work with what we had, but her craft had become fairly limited. It was time to make the investment in the long-arm machine.

Can I just be extra-honest with you for a minute? The idea of going out and spending five thousand dollars on this machine was really tough for me to swallow. I had just finished seminary, we were in a place of financial recovery, and this didn't seem like the most ideal time to make the purchase. Still, I was keenly aware that we had just spent *tens of thousands of dollars* for me to go to seminary, so it really was fair and right for us to invest in this machine that would allow Cindy to grow and prosper in the creative form that she loves so much.

So, we made an agreement: we would buy the long-arm sewing machine, and then she would expand her hobby into a business to recoup the money. That seemed perfectly fair to me because I am entrepreneurial. I have been self-employed for more than thirty-five years, and launching a business is a natural path for me. I neglected to notice that it isn't Cindy's gifting. It's in my blood, not hers. I don't even think about the entrepreneurial spirit because it's so engrained in me, but not everyone has it. Cindy doesn't.

The agreement that seemed so fair and reasonable to me was actually quite unfair and burdensome, but it took me a long time to realize it. I spent months and years checking in on her: I'd ask, "How's your business going?" "How are you expanding it?" "Have you found new clients?" I bought her a camera to take pictures of her work and create a portfolio for interested buyers. But it never got used because photography and building a business are my gifts, not Cindy's. I offered suggestions and ideas. I pestered her for a business plan. She would be evasive, hemming and hawing without any real answers. I had hammered her about this business so many times that she had begun to feel a tremendous amount of pressure.

It took me a long time to come to a very important conclusion. The agreement "to make quilts and prosper" was dividing Cindy's heart and soul. I had created a tension that pulled her in two directions: she wanted to make me happy and try to adhere to the promise, but she didn't want to do tasks that didn't energize her. Cindy's heart had never intended to turn this hobby into an occupation, and I was the one who needed to shift my framework. I could not view the machine as the seed of a quilting business. The long-arm sewing machine was a gift to my wife, to bring joy and delight to her skills and abilities. And the truth is, she is a phenomenal quilter, and she was growing like mad.

So, I released her from the agreement we had made. I set her free from fulfilling her promise. I said, "Honey, I've decided that I am officially taking that expectation off the table. It doesn't exist anymore. I just want you to enjoy quilting, and I want you to learn how to do it better and better, to expand your abilities because *you* want to—not because it needs to bring income to our family."

She didn't believe me. It took her quite a while to accept these words as truth. One reason is because I hold firmly to the belief that you must "let your yes be yes and your no be no" (see Matthew 5:27 in the New Living Translation). I am a person of my word, and I value that integrity in other people. If you make a promise, keep it. I am trusting you to do what you said you're going to do. So, to cancel this agreement with Cindy was counterintuitive to one of my foundational pillars, and she knew that. It was very difficult for Cindy to trust my sincerity. I needed to be intentional to help her understand, with patience and the repeated message. Years later, she's beginning to trust my word. Now I simply delight in what she's good at. I delight in her skills and abilities, and it's my heart's joy to see her do what she loves.

Sometimes delighting in someone really comes down to releasing the vice of expectations. You can choose to love someone for who he or she is, not for what that person offers you. You can choose to delight in your partner's gifts and abilities as an extension of who he or she is, not as a profitable business opportunity. You can choose to delight in the music someone can make, simply because it's a joyful sound, not because the song proves the worth of the lessons.

Release the Expectation

To delight in your beloved is to release him or her from your expectations. You want your beloved to feel respected, honored, and cherished, not burdened under a yoke of requirements or expectations. When you set him or her free and show your delight in your beloved, you will be able to heal some of the wounds from his or her past. When you respect your beloved as an individual worthy of respect, and when you honor that person's place in your life, then you can cherish the color your partner brings to your world.

Respect, honor, cherish. Brass candlestick, wax candle, flame.

Keep that flame burning strong.

TOOL FOR THE JOURNEY:

To delight in my beloved is to release him or her from my expectations. I want my beloved to feel respected, honored, and cherished, not burdened under a yoke of requirements or expectations.

Think about:

- What has your candlestick looked like this week?

- Did you feel the flame going out?

- When was the last time you felt the flame burning?

- Have you been cognizant of sending messages of honor to your spouse?

- Are there any areas of your relationship where you need to release your beloved of the burden of your expectations?

Talk about:

- Ask your beloved:

- o "When and how do you feel most respected by me?"

- o "When and how do you feel honored?"

- o "When and how do you feel cherished?"

- o "When do you feel the flame burning?"

- Ask your beloved if there are any areas where he or she feels burdened by your expectations. Talk about how you may begin to set your partner free.

CHAPTER EIGHT

The Art of Healing

Go Closer to the Grizzly Bear

JAY AND SUSAN HAD been married for ten months when they came to see me. They were fighting a lot, their arguments were escalating, and they could tell their marriage was headed in a direction they didn't want. A lot of people will gasp at the idea of a couple in counseling after only ten months of marriage, but I personally wish I had had that kind of insight and wisdom ten months into my first marriage. (Add that to my list of things I wish I could do over.) Early awareness can be very healthy. I tip my hat to couples who can get to the root of a problem before it gets out of control.

As I discovered their history, I learned that Susan's dad is an alcoholic. I asked her a simple question that's one of my favorites: "What was your relationship with your dad like when you were eight years old?"

She said, "Oh, that's easy. We had an upper-middle-class suburban lifestyle. Dad supported us, and my relationship with him was just fine." That was that, plain and simple. But I suspected there might be something deeper. I asked the same question in a different way in the weeks to come, and I got the same answer two weeks later, and the same answer the next three or four weeks.

About the sixth or seventh week, she came in and said, "I've been thinking about your question." Big crocodile tears rolled down her cheeks. She said, "I've realized that my father was never there for me. I grew up in Texas, where cheerleading is maybe a half step below football, and football is king of the world. I was in competitive cheerleading from the time I was eight years old, and I competed all the way through high school. I even went to state finals twice. My dad never came to a single meet."

Just as I suspected, there was something deeper, indeed. What causes a person to give that first type of answer that Susan maintained for so many weeks? Was it a lack of awareness of her own childhood, or was it a blind loyalty to her dad? Well, it can be both. The emotional barrier works in two directions. It's designed to hide our wounds from other people, but often we hide our wounds from ourselves. Those wounds live in painful places we don't want to go, so we hide from them. It took Susan many weeks to start to realize her dad had not only been absent from her cheerleading competitions; his heart had been absent all along. He had been emotionally unavailable. I could see that she had a fear of abandonment.

Her husband, Jay's, story wasn't one of tulips and rainbows, either. When Jay was fourteen, he came home from school, eager to tell his mom something about his day. He raced up the stairs, burst into the master bedroom, and found his mom in bed with the next-door neighbor. To make that even worse, his family never talked about it. Ever. He learned early on that his family members were simply four separate entities living under the same roof. They occasionally had a meal together, but there was no emotional connection. I could see that he had a fear of intimacy.

Now Jay works in an environment where he needs to interact with women, and let's be honest—it's hard to find a career where you don't interact with the opposite gender. But when Susan would find out about these interactions, it would trigger her fears of him abandoning her, and she would yell and scream at him. She wanted him to promise that he would never talk to another woman, never look at another woman, never engage another woman in any way.

Not only were her expectations unrealistic in his professional world, but her emotional tidal wave made him feel trapped. When she spewed her anger, she would trigger his fears of intimacy, and he would then shut down. She would get louder, and he would back up further. Like Bugs Bunny, he wanted to jump in a hole and pull the dirt in behind him. The further he backed away, the more she feared he was abandoning her and the more enraged she became, until they had trapped each other in a downward spiral. More and more, he felt backed into a corner with nowhere further to withdraw as she came roaring at him like a bear.

This happens often—in many couples, we have the pursuer and the one being pursued. Frequently, the one being pursued has the fear of intimacy, and the pursuer has the fear of abandonment. The pursuer chases, and the one being pursued keeps backing away. They're like two rabbits, chasing each other.

In a counseling session with Jay by himself, I gave Jay a bold suggestion. I said, "When she roars at you, I want you to move in closer to her. Move toward her and give her a big hug."

Jay's eyes grew wide. He said, "Mark, there's no way. You don't understand. When she roars, *she roars!*"

"Jay, you're bigger and stronger than she is. Wrap her in a hug. Whisper in her ear, 'I'm not going anywhere. I choose you. I love you. I'm not going anywhere.'"

His eyes narrowed. "I don't know, man."

"Just try it."

He came back the next week, and he had tried it. Jay told me it was like flipping a light switch. Susan's anger had immediately dissolved when he came closer to her, held her, and reassured her. When he hugged her, it was the greatest act of love he could give her. He gave her exactly what she needed. He fit her puzzle piece perfectly.

Jay filled her void and immediately became much safer for her.

Your amygdala, also known as the "lizard brain," is the almond-sized part of your brain that controls your fight, flight, or freeze responses. Every healthy brain has this defense mechanism, and of course it can serve as a lifesaving defense in moments of true danger. The problem is that the amygdala cannot tell the difference between an actual grizzly bear and a fiercely perturbed wife. Your prefrontal cortex, where your logical thoughts reside, knows the difference between those two. But your amygdala simply tells you there is a present danger and it's time to respond.

Scientists have done studies to show that the prefrontal cortex actually can override the amygdala. You can logically choose a response instead of giving in to fight, flight, or freeze. It's like exercising a muscle, but you have to practice it. When the amygdala launches hormones that start pumping through your body, there is a physical sensation involved. You can feel your blood pressure rising and your pulse racing, and though you may feel as if you're wired to respond only one way, you have the power to recognize those warning signs and respond differently.

The more Jay taught himself to turn toward Susan when she was roaring like an angry grizzly bear, the stronger that muscle became. As he assured her, "Sweetheart, I love you. I'm here for you. I'm not going anywhere," her sense of security deepened. He learned to keep repeating that promise of assurance to his wife, and she began to soften and melt into him.

This practice led them out of the tension they were living in. Jay learned to finish the workday by telling her about any interactions he had with women that day, to explain those encounters to her with openness and vulnerability. In turn, Susan learned how to regulate her fear of abandonment, and she could slow down the process and stop herself before she exploded. Together, they were able to stop grasping for control. As they chose truth and trust, this led them to a thriving relationship. Jay and Susan brought healing to one another.

The Wizard Behind the Curtain

I hope you've seen *The Wizard of Oz*. It's one of the best allegories ever made, and there was a time when I could assume everyone had seen it. I'm discovering that the younger my clients are, the older that movie seems. So, I hope you've seen it, but if somehow you haven't met Dorothy and her friends, add *The Wizard of Oz* to your Netflix queue.

When Dorothy starts off on her adventure down the yellow brick road, she sings, "We're off to see the Wizard! The wonderful Wizard of Oz!" She has heard the Wizard is so wonderful because of the wonderful things he does, and she believes he is the answer to all of her problems. She and her three friends face a lot of travails on the journey, until they finally find the home of the Wizard in Emerald

City. They walk down the hall to meet him, but they're not singing their little ditty anymore. All of their excitement has turned to terror. They see this big, scary, floating head and flames shooting high, and then a booming voice asks, "Who dares come before the Wizard?!"

When they gather their courage, and they ask the Wizard for help, what does he send them to do? He sends them on a journey to get the witch's broom, which is the scariest and most difficult thing they could possibly do. They go through many more travails to get the broom from the Wicked Witch of the West, and now they're ready to take it back to the Wizard. Are they singing their little ditty as they go back down the long hallway? Not at all! They become even more fearful, and the Wizard seems even more powerful.

That is until Toto, the dog, pulls the curtain back to reveal who is actually behind the curtain: a very insecure person. Dorothy is furious, and she begins to react by saying, "You're a very bad man!"

The Wizard, staying nonreactive and nondefensive, says, "Oh, no my dear. I'm a very good man. I'm just a very bad Wizard." Everything changes in that instant. That's when healing begins for all of them. (Seriously, you've got to see this movie. And if you've already seen it, watch it again.)

Emotional barriers can make us seem unsafe and very scary to the people we love. Look at Jay and Susan. When I asked him to turn toward her and give her a hug,

I may as well have sent him on a mission to steal a witch's broom. He couldn't think of anything more terrifying. Perhaps you know how he felt—facing your beloved when he or she won't give you what you feel you need can seem downright terrifying.

Susan felt the same way. The wounds from her childhood had given her the idea that if Jay pulled away from her, she'd surely fall into a gaping, bottomless, black hole. She feared nobody would be there to save her. Giving him space and independence felt comparable to approaching a wizard; there were too many unknown factors, too many ways this journey could go wrong. Our emotional barriers can make us seem unsafe and very scary to the other person.

Some of the wounds and brokenness we have received are like wizards behind a curtain. When you believe there's a powerful force in charge of your life, you can feel out of control and terrified. But when you can see what's hiding behind the curtain, sometimes it turns out there was no wizard there at all.

Now, it's true: other wounds are so deep that they will never be healed this side of heaven. Those are the wounds that require professional help, compassion, and vulnerable conversations. Still, we can each learn to manage those wounds, rather than letting them manage us. Sometimes the choice in front of you feels like the scariest, hardest thing you can possibly do, but it's the path to true healing in your marriage.

The Opposite of Protecting Yourself

Virtually all of my clients say, "I hate confrontations." You know what? I couldn't agree more. I hate confrontations too. I don't like conflict any more than you do. But I can embrace the idea of *engaging* the fight because it invites us into a process of drawing closer and connecting more. When your beloved is coming at you with arrows and rocks, of course your first instinct is to get defensive or fight back. How can you seek to be nonreactive, and instead move closer to the other person? Sometimes it begins with a small step toward a grizzly bear, a posture that feels exactly opposite of what you'd normally do. You want to protect yourself, and you tend to go into preservation mode, but ask yourself: "What if I didn't do that? "

Conflict is inevitable. That is part of God's design. When we handle the conflict the way the world does, we tend to separate, isolate, and fight harder to protect ourselves. But when we handle conflict the way God has invited us to, we can engage the conflict instead of the confrontation, and we can tighten and strengthen the bonds of the relationship.

When Jay whispered into Susan's ear, he was taking a big risk with a small gesture that was against his intuition. But it was extreme and tangible. He had a long-term view in mind, a goal of loving his wife better instead of winning a fight in the moment. That can be the beginning of heart change. It may not happen immediately, as it happened for Jay and Susan, but a small change in your short-term response can be the beginning of long-term healing.

Jay and Susan were able to engage each other to begin to heal and manage the wounds they each carried into the marriage. As a wonderful postscript to this chapter of their story, I am delighted to tell you that after years of infertility, they contacted me to let me know they had a beautiful baby girl. Perhaps their connection healed far more than their emotional wounds. When healing begins to occur, hearts begin to connect. We offer to one another a safer place to share more and more, and the bonds of the relationship grow stronger and tighter.

This is the art of healing.

TOOL FOR THE JOURNEY:

**Conflict is inevitable,
but it does not have to be damaging.
When we handle the conflict the way
God has invited us to,**

**we can engage the conflict
instead of the confrontation,**

**and we can tighten and strengthen
the bonds of the relationship.**

Think about:

- Think of a time when your beloved was coming at you in an argument, when you felt tempted to pull away. What could you have done differently to move toward your partner, not away from him or her?

- If you chose not to retreat and protect yourself, what is the worst thing that could happen?

- What would it look like to engage the conversation instead of confronting your beloved?

Talk about:

- Ask your partner: "What does the grizzly bear in our relationship look like?"

- Ask your partner: "What feels scary or unsafe to you?"

- What would you like your partner to do differently, particularly when you feel triggered?

CHAPTER NINE

The Art of Vulnerability

Create a Safe Space

FOR MORE THAN TWENTY-FIVE years, I have been trying to learn how to read Cindy's mind. I'm no better at it today than I was on the day when we first met. I know her very, very well. She's my better half, the wind beneath my wings, and the best part of my life. Still, try as I may, I cannot read her mind. I frequently have to ask her to fill in the gaps to finish the story. I learned this early on, when I realized too late that I had had no idea that she was mad at me.

Here's how the story developed. When our children were young, Cindy had a special bedtime routine with them. She would spend as much as a half hour with each child, tucking each one into bed. Each child got fifteen to thirty minutes of undivided time with Mom, talking about the ups and downs of the day, reading a story, getting a back rub, and finishing the evening. Bedtime was an important part of her childhood, and she continued this with her children.

In the meantime, I'd go into our bedroom, brush my teeth, crawl into bed, and read a book to slow down my thoughts at the end of the day. About an hour later, she'd come in to bed to find me totally engrossed in my book. I was in my own world at the end of the day, totally oblivious that she needed or wanted anything from me. After a few minutes, she would roll over—angry—and go to sleep.

It all came out in our counselor's office, this error in my bedtime ways. I learned that I had been making a nightly mistake. After each of her children had debriefed her about their day, she came to bed hoping to debrief with me. She had spent an hour listening to them, and she wanted me to do the same with her. She longed for my undivided attention, for me to listen to her ups and downs, to finish the evening with intention. But I was clueless. I had no idea I was hurting her, night after night.

Lack of Information Erodes Trust

When Cindy came to our bedroom to find me reading my book, not exactly waiting to talk to her and hear about her day, she may have thought, *He doesn't even care about me. Who's checking on* my *heart? Why won't he tuck me in?* But I was lacking the information. I didn't even know I had dropped the ball. I was eroding her trust, but I had no idea because I didn't know there was a problem. She thought I was choosing to ignore her, and emotional separation occurred.

Lack of information erodes trust, and in the absence of information, we write our own stories and create our own truth.

Your relationship needs a safe space for each person to speak openly and to feel heard. Without this safe space, we will rush in with our own broken, wounded assumptions, which may be way off base. In this situation, our imaginations are not our friends. Our thoughts run wild, and we pin intentions on the other person that may not be accurate at all. In the absence of information, we write the end of the story, and it may not be the story our partners want us to write at all. They may not even know we're drafting our own ending. When you rush in to finish the story, you've made incorrect assumptions, and the other person has no idea what happened.

In our situation, Cindy couldn't share it with me because I was too intimidating for a tender topic like that one. We hadn't learned how to be vulnerable with one another, so her safest place was in the presence of our marriage counselor. Indeed, I needed to pursue her heart on a number of levels. I couldn't know what was wrong because I hadn't created a space for her to be honest and vulnerable.

As we talk about creating a safe space, I hesitate to say that it's any single person's responsibility—even the person with the stronger personality, who may seem less approachable. I am firmly planted in the idea that there isn't blame for the weaknesses in a marriage, and no one person has greater responsibility for the state of the marriage. It's both/and, not either/or. Yes, I had a role in creating a safe place for her to approach me, but Cindy also had the role of taking responsibility for what she needed to say. When I can listen well, when I choose to not react emotionally or become defensive, then she can open up and be more honest with me. In the same way, when she chooses to not be reactive or defensive, then I can let my guard down. It works both ways as we continue deeper into the spiral that brings us closer to one another.

Each Person Gets a Voice

I'm working with Larry and Margaret right now, and they are very close to retirement. They have maintained a successful business together, and now that they're getting ready to sell it, they're on the brink of becoming multimillionaires. Within the next few years, they'll be able to go anywhere and do whatever they want with all the money they've earned. The world will be their oyster. Sadly, there is no connection between them as they begin to dream, plan, and think about their future together.

Margaret's home is a safe place for her, and she doesn't want to give that up, so it's difficult for her to imagine the possibilities. Quite the opposite, Larry tends toward wanderlust, with big dreams of acreage and boats and land to explore. He's a very successful entrepreneur, so he's used to being in control. Margaret is used to him being in charge, and she isn't accustomed to speaking her wants or needs. They need to somehow merge their paths and begin to think together, and they needed to begin by giving Margaret a voice.

Here is the exercise I gave them as a homework assignment: Margaret gets to talk about what retirement could look like, where she wants to live, and why. Larry's job is to simply listen and draw out information. This is not his chance to respond or react to anything, because this stage is not about making decisions. It is simply a time for an information download. Larry's job is to seek to understand everything Margaret *feels* about this topic, to simply receive her perspective, not to decide if she is right or wrong.

When she has finished, Larry needs to ask, "Is there more?" And I don't mean, "Good grief, woman! Is there anything left you have to say?" But rather, "What more can you tell me about this? I want to hear it all. Give it to me." He needs to keep listening until she finally comes to the end of her ideas. If she says, "Oh, wait; I have one more," then he will keep listening.

When Margaret says, "That's all there is. I cannot think of one more idea," then they switch roles. It is Larry's turn to think out loud, to look off into the distance and dream. But Larry has to be careful; it is his turn to share his dream, not to attack her ideas, thoughts, and feelings. It's Margaret's job to draw out the information, to ask for more, to patiently listen until he has nothing left to say. They are to repeat these sessions until both of them are completely, totally finished.

I'm trying to get them to come together about a topic that should simply be a lot of fun to talk about. Enough of their typical top-down decision-making process, where Larry decides how this will go and his leadership causes separation. Now they will connect as equals. She will speak; he will listen. He will speak; she will listen. As they learn this dance of back-and-forth, listening all the way to completion instead of talking *at* one another, then they can learn to talk about deeper things. This starts with giving each person a voice for as long as he or she needs to speak. This is what a conversation can look like when both people agree that no issue is more important than how they treat one another.

Thoughts Are Not Expectations

We can get these confused on both sides of communication when we forget that thoughts and expectations are not the same thing. Let's use Larry and Margaret as an example. As Margaret is listing her ideas, Larry may be prone to jumping to the end of her sentence or thought, receiving her ideas as a to-do list of expectations. That's why I asked him to sit quietly and listen, listen,

listen. Margaret needs the space and permission to simply voice her thoughts.

On the flip side, if Margaret does not feel confident to share her thoughts with Larry, she may fall into old habits of writing a silent story he knows nothing about. She could think to herself, *I'd like to do a, b, and c, and he'd probably be okay with that because it means he can do x, y, and z. It's a good plan.* She moves forward with her plan without ever saying it out loud, expecting that he is in line with her thoughts. Thoughts are not expectations. This is when confusion happens.

As I continue to learn the patterns and preferences of my beloved wife, I frequently need to ask for more information to clarify what she wants. I may have started the story in my head, but I need her to finish it. Tell me the rest. What am I missing? What did I not get? I need all of those pieces. Often, the problem is fairly easy to solve, when we can both operate with all the information.

So, when I learned in our counselor's office that Cindy was upset with me on a nightly basis, it was kind of a relief. I wasn't relieved that she was upset, but I could solve this problem. Now, when she gets into bed, whatever time that is, I put the bookmark in the page, put the book down, turn and face her, hold her hand, and check in with her. I give her my undivided attention for however much time she needs. Our bedroom at the end of the day is one of the safest places for both of us. We engage, connect, and listen, and she knows she has all of me. Vulnerability has found its home.

TOOL FOR THE JOURNEY:

Lack of information erodes trust.

In the absence of information, we write our own stories and create our own truth.

Our relationship needs a safe space for each person to speak openly and to feel heard.

Think about:

- Are there topics in your marriage about which you need to say to your beloved, "Is there more?"?

- Do you feel there is a safe place for each of you to have a voice and be heard?

- As a couple, are you setting aside time and energy on a regular basis to talk about any and all topics?

- Does your marriage have an environment where your partner wants to hear everything you say and feel?

Talk about:

- Put a time and place on the calendar where you can pour out your thoughts and feelings to each other on a regular basis.

CHAPTER TEN

The Art of Forgiveness
The Superglue of the Relationship

OUR THOUGHTS FUEL OUR feelings, and our feelings fuel our thoughts. They feed one another in a spiral that gains momentum as it spins. Relationships are not stagnant, and they do not stay still. They are living entities, and they are either growing in a positive direction or headed in a downward slope. Your relational spiral can spin upward, into a positive, healthy place with fresh air to breathe and freedom to enjoy together, or your spiral can spin downward into a negative, unhealthy place where all you can see and hear is conflict.

The downward spiral is the natural state of things. Mountain ranges are built up; then they span millennia breaking down. Flowers bloom, but then they wilt and die. It's sad and unfortunate but very true; the natural order of the world is decay. Without intentionality, effort, and energy, things die, even things we love. Building something requires intention.

How can you shift the direction of your relational spiral? How do you get to a place of understanding that the other person isn't the enemy, and how do you keep an awareness that your beloved is simply an imperfect person loving you the best ways he or she knows how?

You do this through confession and forgiveness.

The Choice to Forgive

Whenever someone does something wrong to you, you have two choices. First, you can make that person suffer for what he or she has done, and most people wouldn't even disagree with that motivation. When you have been violated through a loss of your happiness, trust, or security, there is no price tag to put on that loss, and it feels entirely reasonable to make the other person pay by taking away his or her own happiness, trust, and security. Who could blame you? It's a viable choice. But it's one that hurts you in the long run, as you'll only lose more and more of your own freedom as you choose to carry this offense into your future. The darkness of the debt cannot go away, and it will spread into your soul and change the fiber of who you are.

There is another option: you can forgive. Forgiveness means you refuse to make the other person pay the debt for what he or she did to you. Forgiveness feels painful from the start. Agonizing, even. That pain is valid, because you're choosing to hold yourself back from all the revenge you want to do to the other person. You've not only lost a dose of your own happiness, but now you're absorbing more of the hurt by forgoing the chance to inflict the same hurt on the other person. It's no small thing. It's a decision that calls for sacrifice, as you lay down your right to take matters into your own hands.

If I had to pick one, I'd say forgiveness may be the most important practice of intentional love. It's the antidote to all of the harm done in marriage, and it's the superglue that binds us together again. As a couple, we grow closer and stronger every time we choose to practice confessions and forgiveness. It is impossible to love people well without somehow trading places with them, welcoming them into your heart space, and exploring theirs as well. Love is an exchange, and when you exchange hurt for forgiveness, you've strengthened the tie with the one you love.

Why does forgiveness even matter at all, let alone *this much?* A marriage needs to be a safe place in order for individuals to thrive inside the relationship, and forgiveness is a big key to creating safety. When you give a genuine apology to your beloved, you show your understanding of your own brokenness and your inability to love perfectly. When you can admit and alter not only your actions, but—most importantly—the attitude behind your actions, then you can restore your partner's trust in you. You can help each other feel safe again. This is the key difference between a relationship that is thriving and one that is struggling.

Forgiveness is a muscle that grows stronger with practice, which makes it easier to forgive the next time and the next and the next. The more I forgive, the more I trust that forgiveness is a central part of our relationship, and the more I can trust that you will forgive me when I need it too. Forgiveness offers the gift of unity. It gives you the chance to work together, to remove all distractions, and to say once again, "No issue is more important than the love between us."

Forgiveness in Action

Dan and Julie came to me at about the same time as Rick and Rhonda, and both couples had shocking similarities: they were each in their midfifties, and each husband had had an affair with another woman nine years before they came for professional help. The affairs themselves were different: one was a sexual affair and the other was an emotional affair. And though Dan did not have a physical relationship with the other woman, the emotional intimacy he shared with her created a crevasse of emotional distance between him and his wife. All affairs are not equal, but from a counseling perspective, all affairs are damaging to the marriage relationship. We had some work to do.

You might think that a sexual affair feels worse than an emotional affair, but that can be misleading. First of all, an emotional affair can involve even more of a person's heart than a sexual affair, and most sexual affairs begin with an emotional affair anyway. Julie felt betrayed, especially because Dan struggled to name what had happened as an affair. He could admit to having interactions with the other woman, but he couldn't understand the problem with the attitude behind it. There had been an element missing from his marriage, and he felt entitled to fill that void outside of his marriage. He had gotten an emotional fix somewhere else, and that is the definition of an affair. Dan needed to come to a place of accepting in his heart that he had had an emotional affair.

They had not been able to agree on this definition, and that toxicity had spilled into every area of Dan and Julie's marriage. Every time they got into any kind of argument, Julie pulled out this old accusation: "Well, you're the one who had an affair." It caused Dan to feel shame, confusion, and defensiveness all over again, reminding him that she felt he was wrong then, he was still wrong, and he'd always be wrong. Her reminders and his failure to understand the problem would stop all conflict resolution in its tracks.

Rick and Rhonda were a little different. Rick's affair was sexual and explicit, and he fully accepted that he had done wrong. The problem lingered because the woman with whom he'd had the affair had been a direct report in his workplace, and she was still there, reporting to him. Rick needed to come to a place of realizing that this had to stop. Whether he needed to find a new job or change the reporting structure in his current workplace, something had to change. For nine years, he had resisted ending that relationship because he believed it was exclusively a business one. Rhonda felt betrayed and distrusting, ignored and invisible, and she couldn't resist beating him over the head with old memories.

With each couple, we had done several months of work, and we had gotten past some of the lesser issues that were separating them. It became obvious that we needed to deal with the affairs.

My goal, when I am coaching people about confession and forgiveness, is not to give them my words, but to help them figure out how to express their hearts in the confession. In my approach, the greatest challenge is to help people understand and accept the heart attitude behind their actions, and not make excuses. The heart attitude is what was inside of you that said as you made the decision that it was okay for you to take this action. Usually, a person's tendency is to say, "Yes, I had an affair, but if we had had a better sex life, or if you had paid more attention to me, or [fill in the blank with any justification], then I wouldn't have had to do that." That is not an apology, and it doesn't lead to restoration.

On the other hand, if a person can come to his or her beloved and say, "I'm sorry I hurt you. There is no good reason for what I did. Here is the attitude behind my actions that led me to believe it was okay for me to do that, and I understand how that hurt you. I don't want to do those actions anymore, and I don't want to hurt you again. I also understand my attitude that caused me to treat you that way, and I will not let that attitude take root in my heart again. Can you please forgive me?"[2] Now we've opened the door for true forgiveness to happen. It begins with the attitude, which always has a deeper root than the action. When the attitude is in the right place, then the appropriate actions can flow from that well. I knew that's what we needed to work toward.

I coached them through the seven steps of confession and the four promises of forgiveness (which we will discuss at length in part 3 of this book). In my office, I turned two chairs toward each other. I told the husband that he could use notes in front of him to help him remember everything he wanted to say in this stressful moment, but he had to make a lot of eye contact. (*A lot* of eye contact.) I invited him to take his wife's hands and look into her eyes. In each case, when the husband finished apologizing, his wife was in tears. She offered to him the four promises of forgiveness, and then the husband was in tears. When someone offers an apology in a profound and truthful way, when that person has laid his or her vulnerability on the table like a beating heart for all of us to see, then forgiveness is a beautiful and natural response.

They hugged for so long that I suggested maybe I should step out of the room and give them a moment alone. As a marriage counselor, it's a wonderful thing when there is so much healing in the relationship that I begin to feel like a third wheel!

TOOL FOR THE JOURNEY:

**Forgiveness is a muscle
that grows stronger with practice,
which makes it easier to forgive
the next time and the next and the next.
The more I forgive, the more I trust
that forgiveness is a central part of our relationship,
and the more I can trust that you will forgive me
when I need it too.**

Think about:

- What did you learn about confession and forgiveness when you were growing up? Was it considered good, bad, or neutral?

- Consider this statement: "Forgiveness means you refuse to make the other person pay the debt for what he or she did to you." How do you feel about that sentence? Do you agree or disagree? What emotion does it evoke in you?

- Consider this statement: "Forgiveness is the antidote to all of the harm done in marriage, and it's the superglue that binds us together again." Do you agree or disagree with this statement about forgiveness? Why?

- How do you feel when you think about confessing to your beloved? Is it a sign of weakness or strength? Why do you feel this way about confession?

Talk about:

- Share what you learned about forgiveness when you were growing up.

- Talk about what makes confessing and forgiving difficult for you. What would make it easier?

- Is there someone other than your beloved whom you feel needs to confess to you, or do you need to confess and ask for forgiveness? What keeps you from doing it?

PART THREE:

The Nuts and Bolts of Intentional Love
A Manual for Marriage

LET ME TELL YOU about Lance and his wife, Anne. They came to me for counseling because they have lots of conflict in their marriage. Anne looks for ways to control Lance, and then she punishes him when he gets out of line. As a result, Lance has stopped trying to communicate with her, but he found a moment of clarity when they attended a parent-teacher conference recently.

As Lance watched Anne's interaction with the teacher, he noticed they were going all around the mulberry bush as Anne brought up a dozen other topics she wanted to talk about, but they weren't discussing the matter at hand: their child. Anne was running the conversation, but nothing was getting resolved. She was rude and misdirecting—just like she was at home. It was an "aha!" moment for Lance when he realized, "Ohhhh, I see. She treats everybody the way she treats me."

Lance is a financial sales guy. In his professional life, he has to pick up on cues from people. He has to look for ways to read their emotions and body language, to see them clearly and make connections. The success of his work depends on this ability to read people. But somehow, he hadn't used this same skill set to understand his wife more fully. Not only could he see that her behavior was a pattern; he could see that she was driven by insecurity as they talked about their son. As they talked about his behavior in the classroom, she felt her own identity as a parent was under scrutiny. That's what caused her to be so domineering, controlling, and manipulating. He could see this dynamic unfolding, and for the first time in the sixteen years of the marriage, he understood his wife's heart at a deeper level than ever before. Her control was driven by fear.

A year ago, he would have engaged in the same dance steps they'd always followed. He would have been frustrated with her manipulation and control, he would have gotten angry with her, and they would have ended up with no solution and even more emotional separation. But with this new awareness, Lance was able to enter the conversation with a direct question for the teacher. "What needs to happen to make this better, from your point of view?" He was able to get to the heart of the problem, release the tension, and let the best solution emerge.

Very often, I counsel people whose marriages are failing, their children are rebelling, and the foundations of their home are fragile, but in the professional realm, they are exceptionally successful. It's a puzzling concept, but it's often true. They have skill sets that they utilize to relate to other people on a daily basis, but they leave their best skills at the office instead of negotiating, communicating, and loving well at home. I've seen CEOs who can negotiate major business deals, but they cannot navigate the Thanksgiving table with their two grown sons. I've seen women who are counselors or therapists with their own practice, and while they spend hours listening well every day, they forget to listen well at home. Sometimes we give the world our best selves, and we neglect the people who make up the fabric of our lives.

Intentional love involves pouring energy into your marriage, using your gifts and abilities, and seeking to understand what wounds are driving you, all for the benefit of your marriage. Lance had the ability to hear people and to pick up on their physical and emotional cues, but he had rarely applied that same skill set to his relationship with his wife. This runs counter to what culture teaches us about marriage, and that is the "happily ever after" mentality. Fairy tales tell us that the knight wins the damsel, the battle is over, and they live happily ever after. Of course, this is the end of the fairy tale, movie, or book, and just exactly *how* they are able to live happily ever after is never broached. In real life, after we have spent months intentionally wooing this person we're dating, then somehow after the wedding, too many couples stop being intentional—as if the battle is won and all that's left is the "happily ever after." But the truth is, we're just getting started. (It is for this reason, as I mentioned, that I reserve one or two of the premarital counseling sessions for six months after the wedding. Things change when the dust settles.)

In part 3 I want to give you a manual for marriage, complete with the nuts and bolts of what this can really be about on a daily basis. As you read this, you may think, *Well, of course. I do that all the time."* And maybe you do—with people outside your marriage. As I said, we all have skill sets to help us navigate the myriad of relationships in our daily lives. This section will help you bring that collection to your kitchen table.

While we want to be as practical as possible, we are discussing the art of intentional love. Just like any other learning curve, each skill and craft takes practice. If you want to be a painter, you can learn about texture, technique, color tones. If you want to be a writer, you learn about story structure, grammar, and point of view. But as we grow, we have to practice, make mistakes, and learn. Develop your own style. This is where it gets real. I want to put the tools in your hands, to equip you to love better sooner.

CHAPTER ELEVEN

You Make Me Mad

What Kind of Angry Are You?

LET ME TELL YOU a powerful truth you won't like: nobody can make you angry. (Did you just cringe? I understand. It's a hard sell. Stay with me.) When I say this to groups of people in my workshops, particularly in my divorce recovery classes, people disagree with me pretty fiercely. They'll say, "Oh, there's no way that is true. My ex makes me angry every single day." But anger is a choice, and it's only one of many responses you have to choose from.

Anger is a morally neutral emotion and itself is not a sin. In fact, anger is common among us all. It is inescapable. God created anger within our spectrum of emotions. Even the apostle Paul included anger as a reality when he wrote, "In your anger do not sin" (Ephesians 4:26). He didn't say, "Be sure you never feel anger." He actually allowed for the fact that we would feel this emotion, and he simply instructed us on what to do next. Because that's where the problems lie: in what you do next.

Anger is a tool of communication, and it's an indicator of an underlying emotion. The heart of overcoming anger is the challenge of getting to the emotions that are underneath the anger. When anger shows up, it's an emotional barrier that creates space between me and someone or something I don't want to experience. *When I can determine the wound that's fueling it, then the anger can calm down and even disappear. Anger is never really the problem, so we have to identify what the problem really is.*

What Kind of Angry Are You?

In their book, *Overcoming Emotions That Destroy*, Chip Ingram and Dr. Becca Johnson describe three distinct ways that we tend to respond to anger: we *spew it out*, we *stuff it in*, or we *leak it out* a little bit at a time. They call these groups of people *Spewers*, *Stuffers*, and *Leakers*.[3] Sure, there are other resources and specialists with much fancier names for angry behavior, but I like these. They're simple to remember and easy to picture.

Spewers are usually the easiest to recognize, and they can even identify themselves. The motto of the *Spewer* is, "You bet I'm angry."[4] To them, the only way to get rid of anger is to get it out, and they are loud and demonstrative. *Spewers* are direct, and they don't beat around the bush. If they're mad, you know. Their voices get louder, they're prone to cussing, and they have a short fuse and a quick temper. After they spew their anger on the people around them, they are usually filled with remorse or rationalizations— they will either feel terribly sorry for what they've done, or they will explain to you why this outburst was your fault in the first place.

Stuffers put their emotions away. They don't want their anger to show, because they believe anger is a bad thing. They bottle it up inside, keeping a tight lid on their emotions and avoiding it at all costs. People pleasers are often *Stuffers*, and they will ignore their own feelings and risk losing touch with their own emotions because they don't want to risk upsetting another person. They become sullen, withdrawn, and quiet when they are upset. *Stuffers* think they are protecting themselves and others from their anger, but this comes at a high cost— emotionally, relationally, and sometimes even physically. The unintended consequences are damaging to themselves and to their relationships.

Leakers are not quite as recognizable as the first two angry personalities. Similar to *Stuffers,* they don't like to let their anger show, but they also don't want to keep it completely hidden. Instead, they leak it out, just a bit at a time. They may not confront directly, but they will do little things to bother, annoy, and inconvenience the person they're angry with. They'll show their anger in subtle, passive ways. *Leakers* may gossip, make negative comments, and be critical because they're "just being honest." They often keep score of wrongs, and they will make sure to pay it back—one little bit at a time.

Based on my experience through my years as a counselor, I'd go one step further to say that in time, every *Stuffer* becomes a *Leaker* or a *Spewer.* Eventually, you have to do something with all that junk inside you. A *Leaker* or a *Stuffer* may not seem as scary as a *Spewer*, since a *Spewer* is usually a loud person with a large personality, screaming in your face. But I contend that all three styles are equally damaging to the relationship.

We all get angry. Sometimes it is silent, and sometimes it is loud. Personally, I am a *Spewer.* When I get angry at Cindy, I can seem like a large, broad NFL lineman towering over her, trying to take her head off. She weighs half what I weigh, and my physical presence can be very intimidating. (Imagine how our children felt, who were one-quarter of my size back then.) I'm aware of this now, but it took me a lot of years to come to terms with the damage I could create.

In my practice and my workshops, I work intentionally to help women understand their anger style. A lot of them can identify with stuffing, but they usually don't understand that it's just as damaging as the other anger-management styles. We've each got to learn how to engage conflict, rather than avoid it. When we can accept responsibility for the behaviors, thoughts, and feelings expressed in our anger, then we can begin to resolve conflict with one another.

Peacemakers and Peacekeepers

Perhaps you are reading about these anger styles, but you cannot identify with any of them. Maybe you consider yourself to be a peacemaker, one who will give up the argument because peace is more important than winning. You don't like to fight, you're not competitive, winning doesn't matter to you, and you'll lay down your sword every time if it means the conflict will come to an end. I know your type, and I would challenge you on the title. You're not a peacemaker—you're a peacekeeper.

The peacekeeper wants peace at whatever cost, so he or she will do whatever it takes to silence the argument. Peacekeepers cannot tolerate conflict. A peacemaker, on the other hand, will often engage the argument and the conflict, knowing that peace is lying on the other side of this conversation. Peacemakers will wade through the murky waters in order to find the harmony created by finding a real solution that works for all parties. They want to get at the root of what the conflict is about, because they want to establish lasting peace in the relationship. On the contrary, the peacekeeper wants everyone to quiet down, settle down, and find their happy voices again. That is actually a shortsighted view. That kind of peace won't last.

A great number of peacekeepers have come out of an environment where there was a lot of conflict, and no good things came out of that tension. They have become conflict avoiders, and avoiding conflict becomes their idol. They believe that they need to avoid conflict in order to survive, to do whatever it takes to keep people at peace with one another, so they avoid engaging issues. Peacekeeping seems selfless, but it's actually very selfish. It's a mode of self-preservation.

For the peacekeeper, self-awareness is key. Peacekeepers need to ask themselves, "I know I avoid conflict, but why? Why can't I tolerate it? I am not motivated to find a solution. All I care about is that we don't argue, we don't raise our voices, and we don't escalate beyond control. Why is that so important to me?" Healing comes in engaging the issues with an awareness of our own wounds and the wounds of the other person. When we can find answers that work for us, we have experienced the success of solving a problem. That kind of problem solving will bond any team, especially inside a marriage.

TOOL FOR THE JOURNEY:

Anger is a tool for communication.
When I can determine the wound that's fueling it,
then the anger can calm down and even disappear.

Anger is never really the problem,
so we have to identify what the problem really is.

Think about:

- What kind of angry are you? Have you identified whether you are a Spewer, a Stuffer, or a Leaker?

- Which one do you think describes your beloved?

- This week, keep track of the times when you get angry. (Of course, you have to first admit that *sometimes* you get angry!)

  o What did you get angry about?

  o What triggered you?

  o What emotion fueled the anger?

- If you consider yourself a peacemaker, but you are learning you may actually be a peacekeeper, think closely about the following questions:

  o Why can't you tolerate conflict?

  o Why is a peaceful environment so important to you?

  o Is the absence of conflict what you really want most? Or do you want to find lasting solutions to the problems in your relationship, even if it involves discomfort in the pursuit of those solutions?

Talk about:

- Enlist your beloved if you are struggling to identify your methods of processing anger.

- Discuss what you have learned about your anger styles.

- Talk about times when each of you has seen anger enter your relationship recently. How did it make you feel?

- What underlying feelings fuel your anger?

- If you are a peacekeeper, and you prioritize peace at any cost, share why this is so important to you. Identify the underlying fear.

CHAPTER TWELVE

More Than Your Tone of Voice
The Languages of Connection and Separation

"I KNOW EXACTLY HOW to solve this problem."

"No, I heard exactly what you said to me. What you said was . . ."

"You have no idea what you're talking about."

"Why should I ask your opinion? This has nothing to do with you."

"You always hurt me, and you never care."

These are the comments I hear between couples in high conflict in my counseling practice. Let me assume the role of your high school grammar teacher, for just a moment. I promise not to make you diagram these comments for subject-verb agreement, but let's look at these sentences and identify the pronouns these couples are using. Do you see them? *I. Me. You.*

These words may seem harmless, and certainly they can be. I mean, they're just pronouns, right? But healthy marriages are not built on a foundation of *you* and me. Loving intentionally calls us to a new way of thinking with a new set of pronouns: *we, us,* and *ours*.

John Gottman is a leading researcher into marriages and relationships in America, and he was recognized in 2007 as one of the ten most influential therapists of the past quarter century.[5] Gottman has done extensive longitudinal studies with thousands of couples, and he says that if you give him an hour with a couple, he can predict—with 90 percent accuracy—whether or not they're headed to divorce. His metric is the ratio of positive to negative terms they use in reference to one another and their history together. I won't go so far as to claim that kind of predictive ability, but I do know what he's talking about. I can usually tell fairly soon what kind of trajectory the couples are on, and my metric is their ratio of plural to singular pronouns.

Our awareness of how we relate to one another is something we must keep before us all the time, and it comes down to our actual word choices. I call this *the languages of separation and connection*, and I know each when I hear it.

What Language Are You Speaking?

It's entirely possible that a husband and wife may be speaking two different languages. If one person is speaking a language of connection, and the other is speaking a language of separation—or if *both* are speaking languages of separation—then no communication can happen. It's not very different from a household where one person speaks Spanish and the other speaks German. If we have no words in common, no communication can happen.

Here's a basic breakdown of these two languages. Take a look at the differences.

Language of Separation	Language of Connection
Uses singular pronouns: *I, me, you*	Uses plural pronouns: *we, us, our*
"You're *wrong*!"	"We seem to disagree on this."
"What are you gonna do about it?!"	"How can we reach a solution that satisfies both of us?"
"Well, *you* just need to . . ."	"I think our best move might be to . . ."
"I know . . ."	"I believe . . ."
"I heard what you said, and you said . . ."	"If I heard you correctly, I believe I heard . . ."
"You don't know what you're talking about."	"I believe you are mistaken."
"I know what we should do."	"Perhaps one way we can move forward would be . . ."
Driven by fear	Based on love
Needs to win	Desires to delight
Protects self	Respects the other person

Language of Separation	Language of Connection
Grasps for control	Seeks to honor
Requires	Cherishes
Confrontational	Engaging
Seeks power	Demonstrates humility
Blames	Seeks to understand one's *own* role in this separation
Interrupts	Allows the other to finish and acknowledges what he or she said
Gets louder	Uses a calm voice
Makes declarative statements	Asks questions
Makes demands	Makes suggestions
Listens to respond	Listens to hear
Fights over minutiae	Seeks to understand what is important
Long, argumentative texts	Face-to-face communication
Keeps score	Serves
"My perspective is correct."	"I want to understand your perspective."
Hounds the other person for information or answers	Is patient and asks big questions ("Would you tell me more about that?")
Uses absolutes: *always*, never	Uses qualifiers: *frequently, a lot of the time, too often, a majority of the time*

Language of Separation	Language of Connection
Starts sentences with, "I'm too tired to . . ." or "I'm too busy to . . ."	Starts sentences with, "I would love to discuss that with you, but is there another time that works?"
Begins sentences with, "I am not the problem," implying that the other person must be the problem	Responds with, "I can see how I have contributed to this situation," conveying a sense of responsibility for the problem.
Disrespectful and name-calling	Strives to always be respectful in tone and word (the only name-calling that is permissible is a term of endearment without sarcasm)

Look at the column on the left, the *language of separation*. These words —*I, me, my, you*— display an attitude of selfishness. Their responses are filled with singular pronouns, identifying just one person at a time. The language of separation focuses on "you statements," which point a finger at the other person to say, "You are the problem." The language reflects a heart attitude that believes that the other person is the enemy, the issue is most important, and the speaker must do whatever is required to control this situation and *win*. Ultimately, it comes down to the Cookie Monster mentality: "I want what I want, when I want it, how I want it. And in all honesty, I want *you* to enable me to have all of that."

Now compare this to the column on the right, the *language of connection.* These words— *we, us, our* — display a desire to love well and to find answers that work for both of us and for our relationship together. This language is filled with plural pronouns that reflect a heart of unity. A couple who uses the language of connection believes that no issue is more important than how well they are relating and treating one another, even in disagreement.

When a person is speaking the language of separation, he or she is listening only enough to develop his or her response. *A person who is speaking the language of connection is listening to truly hear and understand. This can change everything.*

Therapist's Confession

I hate to say this, but it's true and I need to tell you. (Brace yourself for gut honesty.) I really don't care what my clients' issues are. Every couple can always find plenty of topics to argue about. That is a bottomless well, and it doesn't interest me. I don't like playing judge and jury to whatever you're fighting about. A wife asked me recently, "So, based on what you know of couples who fight like we do, how often do you think we should be having sex?" Listen: I know what she was after. She wanted me to sway the vote in her direction, and I can smell that from a mile away. It's not what I'm about. I don't care how often you're having sex, actually. I don't care about your budget or TV preferences or dinner schedule or household chores. It just doesn't interest me, and it's not why I went into marriage counseling.

What I care about is *how you are treating one another.* That will forever matter to me, and it's why I do what I do. How are you working through the challenges life throws at you? How well are you listening to your spouse? How well do you know one another, and how are you relating to each other? This is what matters to me. Life will never run out of challenges for you, and those challenges will constantly evolve and change—but they will never go away. I want to give you the tools to navigate these challenges, so you can solve your problems on your own. My goal is for you to graduate from my office. I know my practice is effective when you don't need me anymore.

When I teach people about the languages of separation and connection, I give them this good news: *this tool can work in all relationships.* As you watch people interacting in your daily life, you can begin to see what's going on. You can practice developing the eyes to see and the ears to hear what's happening underneath. Ultimately, when a person is speaking the language of separation, that person is protecting his or her own wounds. When you know what you're looking for, you can spot a wound protector from a mile away—and you can begin to see if *you* are one.

Half-Empty or Half-Full?

In my marriage seminars, I frequently hold up a glass half-filled with water, and I ask the proverbial question: "Is it half-empty or half-full?" Everybody assumes that the half-full perspective is the right way of looking at the glass, but that's not the case at all. It's actually a loaded question. The truth is, when you can stop grasping for what you feel you have to have, when you stop being driven by a single-minded focus to win, and when you can seek togetherness instead of separateness, then your cup is neither half-empty nor half-full—it begins to overflow.

At the heart of any argument is usually a basic fear: I'm afraid that I won't get what I think I need, I'm afraid you will get too close to my wounds, and I'm afraid that this will be the end of my life as I know it. (It sounds dramatic, but on some scale, it's almost always true. It's why people argue.) Our fears stand tall around our wounds, and our wounds are constant forces pushing us away from one another, toward separation. When I remember that my woundedness is getting in the way, that it's affecting how I am interacting with Cindy and how well I'm loving her, then I'm more able to keep the right heart attitude. I'm more likely to focus on connecting when I am aware of those unconscious forces that try to drive us apart.

When I am grasping at what I think I really need to win an argument, then I feel fortunate if my glass gets half-full. Cindy ends up giving me far less of what it is that I really want. I have to be willing to sacrifice my wounds in order to pursue what is best for *us*, but so often, my fear gets in the way. When I can release that, and instead seek our togetherness, then I get so much more. I can turn my focus toward Cindy, and when I can see that she feels accepted, cherished, and loved, there's a look in her eyes that fills my cup to overflowing.

The Choice to Be Nonreactive and Non-Defensive

The languages we use are indicative of our hearts. When your beloved acts in a way that's hurtful to you, you have many choices to make. You have a choice of what words you will use, which way you will respond, and whether you will react defensively in ways that fuel the argument, or you can decide you will be intentional about seeking to understand what is driving his or her behavior.

I can tell you right now what's likely to happen: if you're unaware of the fears that are driving you and your spouse, then you'll step right into the arguments you've always had. But if you can take a step back, identify the fears that might be driving the behavior, and name the wounds that drive your responses, then you can choose a different approach. Instead of *I*, *me*, and *you,* choose *we, ours*, *us*.

Many counselors and therapists believe you can address and change behavior at the cognitive level, but

I don't think problems can be truly addressed at the surface level. Heart attitudes begin much deeper, at the level of wounded emotions. When we can address the heart attitude and nurture it in healthier directions, then out of that can come the right thoughts, words, actions, and behaviors. Look deeper. Ask yourself, "What fear is driving me? What fear is driving the other person?"

Instead of seeing your partner as the enemy that is causing you pain, shift your focus. See your beloved as part of the answer to your healing.

Instead of saying, "Why is this happening? Why are you doing this to me?" shift your focus. Ask, "What have I said or done to cause my beloved to act in unloving ways? How can I respond to unloving behaviors, actions, and words in a more loving and connecting way?"

By putting conscious effort into being aware, recognizing, and owning these invisible forces, you can give your relationship the life-giving energy it needs to thrive.

TOOL FOR THE JOURNEY:

**The language of connection—*we, us, our*—
displays a desire to love well**

**and to find answers that work for both of us
and for our relationship together.
A person who is speaking the language of connection
is listening to truly hear and understand.
This can change everything.**

Think about:

- Observe when others are listening to respond instead of listening to hear. (Instead of using their energy to listen well, they are crafting their response.)

    o   What do you notice about the two different types of listening?

    o   How do they look and sound different?

    o   How do others respond?

    o   How do you respond, when someone listens to you only to craft his or her next response?

- Notice the times when you were listening to respond and when you were listening to hear.

    o   Did you see any patterns?

    o   When are you listening to respond and when are you listening to hear with your acquaintances? Coworkers? Your boss? Friends? Your kids? Your beloved?

- Be intentional this week about listening to hear.

  o What did you learn about yourself?

  o What feelings were aroused when you listened to hear, especially in situations where you normally listened to respond? Did you feel as if you weren't going to get to say what you wanted? Did it feel as though you were going to lose the argument? Or, did it feel good? Did you feel you were connecting with others better? Were you able to come to better solutions or conclusions in your interactions? Did you notice any difference in how others responded/reacted to you?

- Pay attention to the interactions of people around you. (You may want to keep a copy of the list with you as you're learning to spot these patterns. You can find this table in the appendix of this book.)

  o What language do you hear: the language of connection or the language of separation, or both?

- Pay attention to your own language. Did you see any patterns?

  o When are you using the language of connection and when are you using the language of Separation with your acquaintances? Coworkers? Your boss? Friends? Your kids? Your beloved?

- Be intentional about using the language of connection more this week.

   o What did you learn about yourself? What feelings emerged?

   o How did it affect your connections with others?

   o Were you able to come to better solutions or conclusions in your conversations?

   o Did you notice any difference in how others responded/reacted to you?

- Pay attention when you notice other people use pronouns to blame, fingerpoint, or separate. How do others respond? How do you respond?

- Keep track of the pronouns you use to blame, fingerpoint, or separate when talking with your beloved.

   o Did you see any patterns?

   o When did you feel more connected?

   o When were you feeling upset, angry or emotionally separated?

- Keep track of how often your beloved uses pronouns to blame, fingerpoint, or separate from you.

  o Did you see any patterns?

  o When did you feel more connected?

  o When were you feeling upset, angry or emotionally separated?

Talk about:

- What have you learned about the two kinds of listening?

  o How much do you hear others listening to respond?

  o How much do you hear others listening to hear?

  o What are your emotional responses to each?

- What have you learned about the use of the two languages?

  o How much do you hear others using the language of separation?

  o How much do you hear others using the language of connection?

  o What are your emotional responses to each?

- What have you learned about using *we*, *us*, and *our* versus *I*, *me*, *my*, *mine*, *yours*, and *you*?

    o   How did it feel for you to use *we*, *us*, and *our*?

    o   How did it feel when your beloved used *we*, *us*, and *our*?

- Discuss as a couple how you want to change the ways you listen. Discuss also the patterns you've identified in which language—or languages—you use with one another.

CHAPTER THIRTEEN

Identifying Wounds
His, Hers, Ours

I GREW UP IN the 1960s in a neighborhood where there were no fences, all the backyards spilled into one another, and anybody's mom or dad could parent anybody's child as needed. We were one big community of interchangeable kids and parents and bicycles and picnics. My pleasant memories are plentiful of those days.

I was probably six or seven when I was playing with my buddy Bobby. Bobby and I were born the same week, and our mothers met in the hospital that week when they were each giving birth to a baby boy. They realized that they lived just a block from each other, so Bobby and I became fast friends as our first years unfolded.

We were playing in the backyard one day while our moms talked in the kitchen, and in our roughhousing, Bobby's dachshund bit me on the shoulder. Of course, I went crying into the house, and this is what I remember most: it's one of the few times my mother took me into her arms. She cuddled me into quiet, cleaned the wound, and took me to the doctor to have it checked. It's one of the warmest memories I have with my mom. She loved me very much, but she wasn't the kind to express her emotions in a physical, tangible way. When she held me in her arms that day, when she soothed away my tears, she offered me one of the sweetest memories of my childhood.

When I was in first grade, I got the chicken pox. I had to stay home from school for five days, and we had a maid who cared for me while my parents were at work. That first day, I spent so many hours feeling b-o-r-e-d. (Keep in mind: this is ancient history. It was before video games, movies on demand, etc.). The week stretched before me, with a lot of days stacking up like this one. But to my great delight, when my mom came home that first day, she surprised me with a Davy Crocket activity book. I remember page after page filled with all these punch-out figures and forts and whatnot. I spent the entire week playing with it. That first day had been so boring, but she had thought of me and brought something to cheer me. To this day, I remember feeling very grateful for that surprise and very aware of her thoughtfulness—her intentional love.

A few years later, on a summer day, a bunch of people from our neighborhood were sitting underneath the tree in our backyard, which happened to be the biggest tree on the street and thereby the gathering place. My adult neighbor Wally was there, I recall vividly. Wally played college football, and he was built big and wide. He was a strong guy, and for whatever reason, Wally decided to pick me up and hold me upside down by my ankles in the tree. Everyone was looking at me and laughing, and it was fairly harmless . . . until I began to slide out of my jeans. I was afraid I would fall on my head, but I was more aware of what would suddenly become apparent to everyone else: I didn't find any clean underwear in my drawer that morning, so I simply hadn't worn any. Hanging upside down, I slipped right out of my jeans and into one of the most embarrassing moments of my life.

I was ashamed and humiliated, crying hysterically as everyone laughed at me. Wally put me down, I pulled my pants up, and I ran into my house, straight into my bedroom. Nobody came to check on me. My mom didn't come, and neither did my dad. I didn't get any comfort in the moments that followed one of the worst scenes I can remember. Nobody told me I was okay and good, and nobody helped me deal with my shame and embarrassment. Nobody.

This does not mean I wasn't loved. I was definitely loved. But I was loved imperfectly.

I've listed these memories here for an important reason: *this kind of inventory can be very indicative of the people we've become, how we relate to others, and how we engage the world.* The fact that nobody came to comfort me in my shame and embarrassment caused me to not want to be emotionally open. I learned a difficult lesson: I couldn't trust that the people close to me would take care of my heart, my emotions, and my feelings. This increased my fear of intimacy, a fear I still deal with as an adult.

I told you the story of my mother embarrassing me for my neon green socks, and while this story is similar to that one, it has a nuance that's a little more complicated: that day in the tree revealed a mistake I had made. Obviously, if I had made a different and better decision that morning, if I had gone to my mom to tell her I didn't have any clean underwear, then the whole memory would have become a non-event. It would have been a fun memory of Wally hanging me in the tree. After all, nobody got hurt . . . just my dignity. But as a result of my poor decision being exposed on that day, I grew into an adult who hates to have my decisions questioned. Making a poor decision implies that I am incompetent, and that is triggering for me, as by now must certainly have become clear. If I am entering a situation where I feel insecure, I have a tendency to become impatient and abrupt, or brassy and cocky. These are an overcompensation for my woundedness.

We tend to do that, as humans. If the way we're reacting to the world isn't working for us, we swing the pendulum all the way to the other end and choose a 180-degree difference in the way we interact with the world. Events like these can whittle away at our self-worth, and they are cumulative in their effects. The new memory may be a small moment or a larger event, but such memories, repeated, begin to pile on top of one another, making small wounds worse and turning weaknesses into defeat. This erosion of self-worth takes its toll, and it will affect how you interact with the world.

What Happened to You?

When I am learning about a person's story, I ask a ton of questions. How did your family handle conflict? How did they nurture you? Did you grow up in a family where feelings were central? Or did you grow up in a home where feelings didn't matter very much?

Look at your individual role in the family. Perhaps you were a firstborn son with a lot of expectations. Maybe a "Junior," named after your dad, born to carry on the family name. Maybe you're the baby of the family, the one whose job is to relieve tension and make everyone laugh. Are you the rebellious one? The one who broke all the rules? Or are you the compliant one, who followed instructions? Are you the peacekeeper or the rabble-rouser? Are you the black sheep or the golden child? This is only the beginning of the list, of course.

One of the most important questions I ask is, "What was the worst illness or injury that you suffered as a child?" I am trying to look at the emotional attachment between the child and the parents. Attachment theory says parents are to provide a secure base of love for their children to go out and explore the world, and a safe harbor for them to come back to when the world beats them up. I am fascinated to listen to the events of childhood and the spectrum of parental responses. This exercise is not meant to demonize anyone's mom and dad. But it helps us to see our parents as human beings, not as Mommy and Daddy on a pedestal. We need to look at them as separate, adult human beings, with strengths, weaknesses, gifts, passions, and woundedness. There will always be things they were good at, areas where they struggled, and ways they loved well or didn't. These aspects and characteristics ultimately shape who we become, create our wounds, and establish our triggers.

Sometimes I'll hear a story of a boy who fell off a bicycle, his parents saw it happen, they came rushing over to scoop him up and take him to the hospital, and on the way home they stopped to buy colorful markers so his classmates could sign the plaster cast the next day. Someone else will tell me a similar story of falling off his bicycle, but nobody saw him fall, nobody came to help him, nobody took him to the doctor, and by the time he got medical attention many days later, he needed surgery to have the bones re-broken and set. I'll hear stories of parents who hovered over their children to protect them from illness or injury, other stories of parents who didn't acknowledge the pain of their children's experiences, and still others who found the sweet spot in between, of responding appropriately, addressing their pain and equipping them to cope.

My childhood was generally and genuinely very positive, but I am now increasingly aware of how emotionally disconnected we always were. I can look back on some of my memories and realize that I craved intimacy that my parents didn't always provide. I've become someone who both craves and fears intimacy.

As a marriage counselor, I talk about the most intimate details with couples and individuals. It's the nature and confidentiality of my work. Just this morning, I was discussing a couple's sex life with them, in quite a bit of detail. I know far more about their private lives than anyone else on the planet, and that's true of most people I see. But on a personal level, I walk the fine line between craving intimacy and fearing it. I want a deep connection, but it feels scary to me when the other person gets too close to my wounds. That's when I shut down and pull away. My heart goes out to people who crave intimacy and yet are scared to death of it. That's a tension I can relate to.

In my own journey of trying to understand myself, I want to take a look at the times when I fail to love Cindy well. I want to identify those driving forces that may have been largely unconscious in my life up to this point, and I want to name them and bring them into the light. When I can understand more about those early years and the events that shaped me, then I can examine my wounds and begin taking responsibility for what I bring to our marriage. You can follow a similar path of seeking to understand what forces drive you so that you too can take more responsibility for what you bring into your relationships.

Be Aware of Your Partner's Wounds

Years ago, I worked with Barbara and Patrick. Barbara had an Italian heritage and a big personality, and she spoke with her hands. She was an avid storyteller, a fierce communicator, and she gesticulated wildly with her hands. I mean, *giant* hand motions. If you held her hands, she likely wouldn't be able to talk! Meanwhile, her husband, Patrick, had been raised going to Catholic schools with old-fashioned nuns who literally ruled their classrooms with wooden rulers. During the decades of his childhood, it was a great weakness to be a child who wrote with his left hand, and Patrick was unfortunate to be born in the day and age when his dominant hand was considered an academic failing. Patrick remembered getting rapped on the arm, the hand, or across the knuckles as the nuns forced him to hold the pencil with his right hand.

Whenever Patrick and Barbara got into a disagreement of any kind, she would use her giant hand motions. She didn't mean it as a physical threat, but something about her motions triggered Patrick into feeling as if he were dealing with the angry nuns again. And whenever Patrick felt this memory, he shut down. All of their communication came to a dead end every time. They were getting nowhere as they tried to work through any conflict or disagreement.

The solution for Patrick and Barbara was this: when they had something to talk through, Barbara would begin by sitting on her hands. She physically put her hands underneath her thighs before they began the conversation. With this small sacrifice on her part, she was able to keep from inadvertently upsetting Patrick. It wasn't her fault that she talked with her hands, and it wasn't his fault that he had wounded memories of angry teachers. But her behavior was easier to adjust than his memories were to erase, so this worked for them. It carried them to a place where they could begin to communicate better, since they could finally engage the conversations that needed to happen.

We all have recordings of old memories that play in our minds. Like Patrick, your tape may be of a strict teacher who was hard on you, or perhaps a coach whose expectations were never attainable. Or, like many people who've been married and divorced, you may have the tape of your previous spouse playing in your head. You have the "ex-husband tape" or "ex-wife tape" on a repetitive loop, and it may cause you to respond to your beloved partner the same way you reacted to your former spouse. In moments like these, when you realize you're operating in old patterns of a relationship you're no longer in, it's helpful to have a gracious awareness to say, "I'm sorry; can we start this conversation over? I feel like you're acting as if I'm your [ex, sister, mother, father, abuser, neglecter, etc.]. Let's back up the conversation and do it again, but this time, keep in mind that I'm me. I am not that person."

Sometimes, a simple change can deepen your awareness of your partner's wounds and triggers. Other times, you may need the help of a counselor to identify what these might be. We know that people who suffer from trauma or PTSD can be triggered by a tone of voice, body language, a specific word, a setting, or a scent in the air. If you can avoid tripping the wires that trigger his or her reactivity, then you can do a better job of honoring, cherishing, and respecting your partner. You can be a healthy, healing force in your partner's life when you are not activating old wounds, even by accident.

The Key Element Is Understanding

In order to love Cindy to the best of my ability and with everything I have, the key element is understanding. I need to understand myself, I need to understand her, and I need to understand the basic principle that we keep returning to: I can't love her perfectly, and she cannot love me perfectly. If I can just understand those truths, then grace and mercy can begin to flow in us and through us.

Jesus came to us as a man, and He lived life as a human being. This makes him unique in all religions. He was fully human and fully God, so He understands me. Out of that understanding, grace and mercy flow through

Him. Humility leads us to interact with other people with that kind of grace and mercy, because we can understand who they are and what drives their behavior. When I can understand who my wife really is, instead of who I want her to be, then I can understand when she's operating from the other side of an emotional barrier that's designed to keep me away. I can join her, rather than confront her.

These are the choices that strengthen and tighten the bonds of the relationship, and they lead to exponential growth in wisdom and intimacy. They are rooted in understanding who I am, who she is, who we are together, and who we are not and will never be. Ultimately, we cannot love perfectly, but we can choose one another. We can seek to love better with this awareness. Out of conflict, we can have the humility of spirit to look at our own lives, identify the patterns, and take responsibility for them.

Acknowledge your wounds. Recognize your beloved's wounds. Practice understanding. These are the bonds that bring you back to one another, again and again.

TOOL FOR THE JOURNEY:

A personal inventory of difficult memories can be very indicative of the people we've become, how we relate to others, and how we engage the world.

Think about:

- What was your role in your family of origin? Were you the rebellious one, the responsible one, the golden one, the spoiled baby, the outsider or detached one, or the obedient one?

- What was your relationship like with your father? mother? siblings?

- Were there grandparents or significant others who lived with you and added another dimension to relationships? How did that impact you?

- Were there any addictions to alcohol, drugs, work, sex, etc.?

- How do you think you were perceived by others in your family?

- Think about other significant relationships:

  o Were you involved with others who were a lot like your dad? your mom?

  o Can you see a pattern of relating that runs through your relationships?

- How do you think these have impacted the way you relate to the people in your life?

- What recordings or "voices" do you hear in your head from earlier conversations with your mother, father, previous spouses, or significant others?

- If appropriate and possible, talk with other people who knew your family—maybe aunts, uncles, long-term family friends—to gain their perspective.

Talk about:

- Pick a relaxed setting with no time pressures. You may need more than one session.

- Choose one of you to go first. Share your memories, feelings, thoughts, stories, and other relationships that you define as significant from your childhood.

- The listener's role is to hear and not judge. The listener may ask clarifying questions, but he or she must stay focused on the person who is sharing. Good questions include, "Tell me more about that," or "Is there more?" or "I'm sorry; I didn't get that. Would you tell me it again?" The listener should not share his or her history yet.

- If you begin to feel overwhelmed, stop. If this occurs, the listener should simply be present, possibly hold your hand or wrap his or her arms around you. The goal is not to "get through" this. The goal is to process and discover more about yourself, your woundedness, your brokenness, and what drives you in relationships. Sometimes you may just need a few minutes to recover before you can continue, or you may need to set another time to continue.

- Remember: the one who is sharing is offering up that individual's most precious possession—his or her their heart. Be mindful to treat this wonderful gift with kindness, gentleness, and respect. When the one sharing has finished, or if he or she needs to take a break and wants the other to take a turn, then switch roles.

- Discuss what you have learned about yourself.

- Discuss what you have learned about the other person. Include any new understandings you have of who the other really is or who you have wanted that individual to be.

- Discuss ways each of you loves the other imperfectly. Try to identify triggers:

  o Are there things you "have to have" from the other?

  o Are there things the other wants from you, but you find difficult to provide?

  o What habits trigger the other person?

CHAPTER FOURTEEN

Landmines and Triggers
His, Hers, Ours

CONFLICT CAN FEEL LIKE a trail of falling dominoes. One person makes a comment, the other person responds, emotions heighten, voices rise, and you can begin to wonder how you ended up in this mess. When it happens over and over again, about the same topics or in the same scenarios, there may be some identifiable patterns in place. Sometimes it helps to know which domino was the first to fall, triggering all the rest.

Let's look at Matt and Karla. They have been married for eighteen years, and this is the second marriage for each of them. They are social drinkers, enjoying the occasional beverage with friends at a dinner or cocktail party. Normally, this isn't a problem for them, except for one thing that happens from time to time. Karla has a mannerism that only emerges when she has had one too many drinks, and it triggers Matt to remember living with his first wife, who was an alcoholic. When he sees this mannerism, he goes into a defensive, self-preservation mode. It's not because Karla has done anything wrong, necessarily, but rather he's thinking of his first wife, expecting the night to go downhill until they are alone, when all hell will break loose into a full-blown nightmare.

A trigger can be anything. As we mentioned earlier in the book, it can be activated by a memory, a sound, a song, a person, a joke, or even a scent in the air. In Matt's case, the trigger is a very subtle mannerism that might go unnoticed by anyone else. These moments activate memories of old, painful feelings, and they evoke a strong emotional response. It feels instantaneous, and one domino topples over another and another. With practice and awareness, however, we can each begin to identify that first domino in out scenario and catch it before they all fall down.

Identifying the Triggers

When the amygdala kicks in, there are physical sensations that follow. It feels instantaneous, but it's a process that unfolds: the trigger occurs, the amygdala responds, and then all the hormones spread throughout the body. This doesn't happen all in an instant, and there is time between the trigger and the reaction. *We each need to learn to identify our own triggers as well as our partners'. With practice, we can begin to learn, recognize, and identify situations that are more triggering than others.*

The following exercise is designed to help you identify and understand the dynamic going on between the two of you.

- Think of a recent argument or conflict you had with your beloved. Let's break it apart, moment by moment, and see if we can identify the cause. To understand the dynamic, we will look at the situation from four angles: the behavior, the thought process, the feelings, and the trigger(s).

- First, look at the behavior. What were you doing when the argument began? Were you washing the dishes, brushing your teeth, watching TV, putting gas in the car, starting a load of laundry . . . what were the specific details?

- Next, consider what you were thinking about when something caused tension and/or separation between the two of you. Can you recall what you were thinking as your partner introduced the topic? Where did your thoughts take you?

What were you feeling? This may be difficult to identify, because emotions can be hard to name. Did you feel attacked? Worried? Afraid? Criticized? Concerned? Before you felt angry, another emotion was hiding beneath. Try to identify which one it was.

Finally, what triggered you? What made you start to pull away from the other person?

What caused you to put up your protective barrier? What caused you to create space between you and your beloved?

Practicing the Process

Matt has learned to remind himself that Karla is nothing like his first wife, and an extra drink in her hand will not turn her into his first wife. They are not the same women. Karla is not going to get overly drunk, and she is not going to become irate when they get alone. With logical thought processes, he can override his panic when he draws the connection between the two.

Along the same lines, Karla has learned to turn down the offer for one more drink. She's learned to stop before she drinks enough alcohol to make Matt concerned. That doesn't mean she's perfect, and it doesn't mean that his triggers are her responsibility. Once again, it is a both/and situation: Matt has worked on his response, and Karla continues to avoid tripping that wire or putting a landmine in his path for him to trip on. That's what a healthy relationship looks like.

In my own marriage, I want to learn to identify my landmines and triggers, but I also need to understand and identify Cindy's as well. I don't want to trigger a response in her, and I don't want to cause her to feel as if she needs to pull away from me to protect herself. As I continue to learn to love intentionally, I want our interactions to always pull us closer to each other, instead of causing separation that draws us apart. I want to stop that first domino instead of watching all the dominoes fall.

Looking back on the Phoenix incident, I needed to get in touch with the fact that I was afraid to look incompetent. That's what was fueling my anger, and I couldn't see the truth: Cindy didn't see me as incompetent, and nobody else on the road was even aware of whether my turn was the right one or not. I needed to see how irrational it was to fear that incompetence, since it really didn't matter at all. Once I identified that, I took away the energy that fueled the anger.

We have since found a solution to that GPS problem, by the way. If Cindy is navigating, I will not take the car out of park until she tells me she's ready. It's a "big sacrifice" on my part, since it takes forty-five to ninety seconds for the app to boot up. When Cindy says she's ready to go, then I can say I'm ready to go. It's not that difficult, really, and that minute or two can make all the difference. It helps me stay in the present, rather than going to all the crazy places my mind can go.

TOOL FOR THE JOURNEY:

We each need to learn to identify our own triggers as well as our partners'. With practice, we can begin to learn, recognize, and identify situations that are more triggering than others.

Think about:

- Recall an argument with your beloved. Look at it from every angle:

  o What were you doing?

  o What were you thinking?

  o What were you feeling?

  o What triggered you?

Talk about:

- Share your awareness with your partner and ask for his or her discoveries as well.

  o What was your partner doing?

  o What was he or she thinking?

  o What was he or she feeling?

  o What triggered your partner?

- Keep track of the answers that emerge over time as you repeat these conversations together. You may begin to notice patterns that can be avoided or eliminated altogether.

CHAPTER FIFTEEN

That Is Not Okay with Me
How to Set Boundaries

I LIKE THE OLD adage "Good fences make good neighbors." What does a fence do? It marks a property line with a physical boundary. The property line was always there, even without the fence, but it was vague and unclear. Once you put up a fence, now there is no confusion about where the property line is. If you try to cut across that boundary line, you'll hit the fence. Fences are good boundaries.

I do a lot of work with couples and individuals who are learning to set boundaries and establish rules and consequences. Boundaries are important in any healthy family system, including in one's relationship with the kids, the in-laws, the grandparents, or the husband and wife. It can be difficult for some people to identify healthy boundaries, especially if a family member has been violating your boundaries for most of your life. It can be confusing when you haven't been taught about respecting yourself enough to maintain healthy boundaries. Healthy boundaries do work, but people who have never established healthy boundaries have a hard time getting over the hump of setting them for the first time.

Even if setting boundaries may feel foreign to you, you probably operate within a set of boundaries all the time. Life gives us consequences. It's a natural part of being a human being on this planet. You make choices, and you get consequences. They're not always negative, but they are consequences nonetheless. For example, I love golfing. I'd always rather be golfing than meeting with clients in my office. But since I'm not a professional golfer on a PGA tour, the golf course doesn't pay me to show up. If I don't go to work, I don't get paid. If I don't earn my paycheck, and if I don't then pay the mortgage, then Cindy is unhappy with me.

If you don't show up for work, your boss will not pay you. If you drive too fast down the highway, the police will give you a speeding ticket. Since healthy boundaries are mutual, there are also boundaries for what your boss may require of you and how the police may confront you during a traffic stop. There are consequences to the decisions we make, and these are what empower us to learn how to make decisions in the world. We test the boundaries, and we discover that we either like or don't like the consequences, and then we make our next decisions accordingly.

When you are setting healthy boundaries, you are essentially trying to establish a working relationship with someone who is being controlling, defiant, difficult, demeaning, or emotionally reactive. The definition of a working business relationship is one that is free from emotional reactivity, and the interaction is courteous and respectful, seeking solutions. A simple example of a working relationship may be your interaction with the grocery clerk. When you go to the grocery store, you expect the clerk to ring up your merchandise with the correct price. If he or she rings up your asparagus for $9.99 instead of $0.99, you simply point out the error. You don't yell and scream at the grocery store clerk if he or she makes a mistake. Most of the time the clerk will correct it on the spot. That's because we have a protocol for relating to one another, a social contract that we both abide by.

What Are Boundaries?

Boundaries reflect the truth: you have worth, value, and rights. They are designed to protect your personal space on many levels: physically, emotionally, cognitively, and spiritually. Boundaries give us a framework for dealing with a situation positively. Let's begin with what they are not, since that's where most people's misconceptions lie.

- *Boundaries are not mean and nasty.* You are not a terrible, selfish, mean person for setting boundaries in your relationships. Women in particular feel as though they're being mean when they begin to set boundaries, and this is because in many cases they've never been allowed to set them before. They've rarely been allowed to say they're being run over, let alone to ask someone to stop.

- *Boundaries are not punishment.* When you set a boundary with someone, you are not reprimanding that person for his or her behavior. Punishment focuses on the past, and it's done out of anger. It is designed to extract justice, and that is not what boundaries are for. You are not punishing someone for a misdeed, but you are showing him or her what is healthy and appropriate in a relationship with you.

- *Boundaries are not reactive.* When implemented most effectively, boundaries are a decision made in advance, not a response to poor behavior or negative interactions. It's like a contract. If you act in this way, then this will happen. It's your choice, and you are empowered to make your own choice.

- *Boundaries are not intended to harm.* They are a path to healthy relationships.

Now let's look at the flipside of each of those, to investigate what healthy boundaries are:

- *Boundaries are respectful to both people involved.* They cultivate an environment of healthy, peaceful conversation, where each person feels empowered to influence the relationship.

- *Boundaries are disciplinary.* How is this different from punishment? Well, discipline is focused on the future, and it is motivated by love for the other person. When you discipline someone, you are teaching for the benefit of their learning. We can teach the people around us how to have healthier relationships with us, and we can do that with clear expectations and consequences.

- *Boundaries are proactive.* They allow you to set limits before issues escalate, instead of reacting in ways that can be negative or out of control.

- *Boundaries are all about helping relationships become healthier.* When each person feels empowered with a voice and ability to make his or her own decisions, then relationships can thrive.

How to Set Healthy Boundaries

Amy was in her forties when she came to me for counseling. She said, "I cannot take my dad anymore. He's been so negative. My whole life, he's been critical of me, but it's recently gotten out of control. The truth is, he's critical of everyone—not just me. He criticizes my husband, our children—everyone. He's always been that way. I can't deal with it." Amy needed to establish boundaries with her father, and the path would not be easy. There is a formula for healthy boundaries, and it looks like this:

First, define what the problem is. I told Amy, "You need to tell him that he cannot be critical of you anymore. Tell him that you do not like or appreciate how critical he is, and you need that to change."

Describe the desired change. She needed to tell him what she wanted. She wanted him to either approve of her life choices or stop telling her everything he felt she was doing wrong. If he couldn't agree with the life she had created, then she wanted him to bite his tongue and stop telling her every offense. The desired change was, "You cannot be critical of me to me, my family, my friends or our relatives."

Decide on the consequences or incentives. Amy and I decided on this boundary, "If you are critical of me or anyone in my family, the children and I are going to disconnect from all communication with you for three days. The second time it happens, we will disconnect for five days. The third time, seven days."

Communicate clearly, unemotionally, and preferably in writing. Amy went to her father right before Thanksgiving, and she set her boundary using the "club sandwich" approach. A club sandwich has three slices of bread: top, middle, and bottom. After each layer of meat, lettuce, or cheese, we find another layer of bread. In this parallel, as we establish healthy boundaries, each of those slices of bread represents the repeated message: "I want a healthy relationship with you." As the other person responds with his or her behavior, you respond with your "piece of bread": "I want a healthy relationship with you." With the "club sandwich" approach, you repeatedly communicate your heart's desire to have a better, healthier relationship with the other person. This message should infuse all communications about healthy boundaries.

Amy was not angry, she did not raise her voice, and she was unemotional. She wrote her requests in a letter in which she explained that she loved her father and wanted a better, healthier relationship with him, but she could not continue the way they had done it. When she presented him with her boundary, he immediately disconnected. This is typical, by the way. It's to be expected. People don't like to be told what they cannot do, and they will respond to your boundary with their own.

It's okay. Expect this response. Let the other person be distant if he or she chooses. Respect yourself enough to allow the distance and silence the other person wants. This is why I like the boundary to be communicated in written form. Now, Amy's dad can refer to the message in writing and see if she is acting consistently with what she said she would do.

Reward or discipline as behavior dictates. When Amy's dad connected again, he was critical of her once again. It was time for Amy to follow through with the plan. She said, "Dad, I've asked you not to do this to me. I'm really going to miss talking to you for the next three days. I'm not mad at you, I'm not reacting, but I am disconnecting, as I said I would in my letter. When we talk again, I hope you won't choose to be critical again, or I'll have to disconnect for five days. That would be really disappointing, and I don't want to do that. Dad, I really want a better and healthier relationship with you."

She imposed the consequences immediately, within the same hour, and she disconnected for three days. His criticism came on Tuesday afternoon at four o'clock, and she committed to herself that she would disconnect until Friday afternoon at four o'clock: a full seventy-two hours. When three days passed, she picked up the phone to call him and connect again, but he chose not to answer the phone. Again, this is to be expected. To punish her for imposing a boundary, he chose to make her wait three days for him to respond. People like and need to explore their own empowerment in boundary setting, and this kind of reciprocal response is very normal.

They finally connected again just before Christmas, and he was critical yet again. She had to keep her promise and enforce the consequences, even though these five days extended through the Christmas holiday. It was difficult and it broke her heart, but Amy and her dad didn't spend Christmas together. Sadly, it still wasn't enough. He was critical of her again at the beginning of January, so Amy then set the consequences for seven days. She had to go through this process three or four times before he began to see that she was serious about the boundaries in place.

Allow the Tiger to Attack

When you begin to set healthy boundaries, you're attempting to put a wild tiger in a cage. Tigers don't like cages; they like freedom. People are the same way. At first, we react strongly (and sometimes loudly) to any boundaries set around us. When you put up the walls of this cage, you have to expect that the tiger will react and attack your cage.

This is not just a metaphor. It's true of real, live tigers. If all the bars of the cage are made of stainless steel, if the bars are nonreactive and they don't bend under pressure, then the tiger will still attack the cage, but he will realize soon that the bars don't move. He will eventually stop trying to break them. However, if even one of those bars is made of bamboo, then the tiger will almost kill himself attacking the bars and trying to escape. If there is any chance he'll find his way out, he will never stop trying.

His behavior will only escalate. Think of the last time you went to the zoo. What were the tigers doing? Sleeping. They had learned to lie down and stop attacking because they'd learned that their boundaries are secure.

In the same way, you need to stay nonreactive and immovable when you set your boundaries, just like stainless steel bars. The other person will do many things to test your boundary—he or she will try to go around you, over you, or straight through you. But you just have to keep holding the boundary and impose the consequences every time the other person violates it. You have to allow the tiger to attack the cage, and you must trust that the tiger will lie down.

If you remain consistent, then the other person will decrease his or her reactivity, lulling you into believing that your work is done. Then you begin to let your guard down, and as soon as that happens, there will be an increase in reactivity as the other person attempts once again to lure you into the old, familiar relational dynamic. In this middle stage of boundary setting, you will feel again that this is awfully hard work, and perhaps that you are being mean and nasty. But this is the stage where it is critical that you maintain the boundary by implementing consequences every single time there is a violation.

You see, that last step is where the plan usually falls apart for most people. When you see the other person begin to react, you may feel scared and tempted to give up on setting boundaries at all. It's one of the biggest emotional hurdles that people need to climb. They feel as though they're risking the relationship altogether, but in all the years I have taught this approach, I've never seen that happen. I'm not saying it's not possible—it's absolutely possible. The other person could decide "I'm out of here," but I've never seen that happen. The key is to have—and hold on to—your effective consequences.

As we look at Amy's story, I think we can agree that she had to work hard to maintain her courage and stick to the plan. Amy was scared to death she would lose her relationship with her dad, but she couldn't live in the relationship they had. A lost relationship would be better than what had been going on. She held her boundary, trusting that the tiger would eventually lie down.

The following January, Amy sent me an email to say, "Mark, I wanted to tell you that I've just had the best Christmas in all of my forty-four years. My dad was wonderful. He knew the boundary, and he kept it. He was positive, affirming, and so enjoyable. It's the best Christmas I can ever remember." This is the mature stage of boundary setting. You will feel relief, safety, and as if a heavy weight has been lifted off your shoulders. You will feel more relaxed in your interactions with the other person. You will feel empowered and respected, both by other people and by yourself. You will feel joyful because you now have a better, healthier relationship with an important person in your life.

With effective and consistent consequences, boundaries work.

What Do Healthy Boundaries Look Like?

Think of the differences between coming near a bunny rabbit, a rattlesnake, and a mule. A bunny rabbit is soft, furry, gentle. If you are like me, you would be happy to hold a bunny and keep it close to you. A rattlesnake is intimidating, coiled, ready to attack. You want nothing to do with its bite and its venom. A mule is stubborn and resistant, and a smart person will keep distance from the rear legs and hooves of a mule.

In this analogy, a bunny rabbit represents someone who seeks truth and solutions for everyone involved. A rattlesnake is someone who seeks to control and win situations. And a mule is someone who is defiant and occasionally aggressive. With both rattlesnakes and mules, we must be absolutely rigid with the boundaries. With the bunny, we can be flexible and open, because we share common goals of wanting to find solutions and truths that work for everyone involved.

Healthy boundaries stop undesired behavior. They clearly define what healthy behavior looks like, and they state the consequences of violating those boundaries as well as the incentives for good behavior. Sometimes they can be flexible, and sometimes they need to be rigid.

When Your Boundaries Are Violated

Most people who are inexperienced in setting healthy boundaries may have a hard time recognizing the violations, but as you grow in your ability to love yourself and to understand what boundaries need to be established, then you will recognize the feeling of having your boundaries violated. A violation of your boundaries means you are not being loved well. Probably the most important element is that you have been disrespected. You will have a sense of being personally violated, either physically, emotionally, cognitively, or spiritually. You have been treated as not having great value, and the truth is unarguable: you *do* have great value.

Violations fit into two categories. The first category is the *obvious violation*. Examples include too much "innocent touching." It could be from anyone, but let's say it's a member of the opposite sex who stands too close to you, lays a hand on your forearm or shoulder, or puts his or her arm around you at inappropriate times.

Another obvious violation is when another person is trying to control you with anger or intimidation. His or her anger may be spewing or passive-aggressive, and it is not because you have been unkind or hurtful, but simply because you have been taking care of your own wants, needs, and desires.

Another obvious violation is when the perpetrator is trying to control you, either with money or with rules. You may have a spouse who keeps all the information about the finances and doesn't share that information with you. That is a boundary violation, since spouses should have equal information in order to join together in handling finances.

The other category is the *subtle violation*. These are more difficult to identify, but it is important to be on the lookout for them. In-laws, grandparents, or other well-meaning people may subtly violate your boundaries by giving unsolicited advice you haven't asked for. They may give gifts or assistance with strings attached. They may try to nose into your business as a couple or try to drive a wedge between the two of you.

We talked about the obvious violation when a spouse controls the finances, but a subtle violation may be with a spouse who controls the time or the resources. I have a client who is extremely active in a number of sports, so virtually every night of the week, he is out with his various teams and clubs. His wife is left at home while he manipulates the use of time, money, talents, and resources.

When someone has violated your boundaries, a number of different emotions may surface. You may feel:

- uncomfortable

- controlled

- frustrated

- tense when you think of interacting with that person

- demeaned, because boundary violations are demeaning by their very nature

- like second-guessing yourself about decisions you make

- as if something isn't right, but you can't put your finger on it

It will feel like hard work to establish boundaries in the relationship. You will have to be on guard and alert to recognize when the boundary is being violated. When you're feeling as if you may lose the relationship, ask yourself this question: "Would no relationship with this person feel better than what I currently have?" If that is the case, then yes, you will lose the old relationship . . . as you knew it. But the good news is that this loss will create space to replace it with a new and better—and healthier—relationship.

The Rules Apply to Everyone

I first met Josh and Megan a few years ago when they came to me for some help with their family dynamics. They had twin daughters who were ten years old at the time, and their younger son was six. There was a lot of yelling in their home, and Josh and Megan were having a hard time parenting together because of all the yelling and screaming. I knew we needed to work together to set some boundaries.

They followed the same steps that I outlined earlier in the chapter. They brought their three children together for a family meeting, and Megan said, "Your dad and I have decided there is too much yelling in our family, and we want to hear softer, kinder voices in our home. Starting today, anyone who yells at anyone else will have to spend ten minutes in the time-out chair in the living room." They made a card with the rule and the consequence, and they posted it on the refrigerator. With the new boundary in place, they watched and waited for a reason to follow through.

The next day, Megan was driving her son home from soccer practice when she called Josh to talk about the dinner plan. While she was on the phone, and while the minivan traveled down the highway, she was shocked to feel a sudden gust of wind from the passenger's side. Her son had taken off his seatbelt, gotten out of his seat, and opened the sliding door of the minivan!

As you might imagine, Megan panicked, which caused her son to panic and start yelling. She began squawking, "WHAT IN THE WORLD ARE YOU DOING?! WHAT IS HAPPENING?! GET BACK IN YOUR SEAT! NOW!" She hung up in a fury without saying goodbye to Josh, pulled the car off to the side of the road, and got out to close the sliding door. Hell hath no fury like a mother whose child almost falls out of a moving vehicle.

When Megan had restored the safety of the minivan, she got back in the driver's seat to drive the rest of the way home. In the meantime, she called Josh to tell him about the emergency, and he said, "Honey, I'm sorry to tell you this, but you yelled."

"Well, of course I yelled! Are you kidding me? The door of the car flew open! What would you *expect* me to do?!" Megan could feel her voice rising all over again.

"But we have a new rule," he said, with a calm voice that surely irritated her.

Megan absolutely couldn't believe how this was playing out. Yes, there was a new rule posted on the refrigerator. Yes, a person who yells must spend ten minutes in the time-out chair. But never did she think *she* would be the first one to test the consequences!

When they got home, Megan and her son *both* went straight inside to the time-out chair as a consequence for their yelling in the car. One of the daughters came downstairs to see this unprecedented phenomenon, and she raced back to get her sister. "Come here! Come here! You *have* to see this."

Her twin sister came to the stairwell landing to see what all the fuss was about. She peeked around the corner to see her brother in the time-out chair, which was absolutely nothing out of the ordinary. "What's the big deal? He's always in time-out."

"No, look again! It's MOMMY."

She looked again, leaning farther around the corner this time, to—sure enough—see her mother sitting there, a prisoner of her own choices. And that was the moment when the boundary became real for all of them. It was a turning point for their whole family system, as the parents proved they were not above the consequences and the children realized that the rules applied to everyone.

With effective and consistent consequences, boundaries work.

The Strength of Feeling Empowered

Boundaries can feel very empowering—both for the one setting the boundaries and the one receiving them. Researchers have done studies with children attending elementary school with a playground along a busy street. Without a fence, the children will stay close to the school building. But if you put up a nice, sturdy fence by the road, everything changes. You and I both know that only a concrete wall would be able to keep a car from busting through, so the sense of security isn't foolproof. But the same is true with boundaries: you can't make a person change his or her behavior. You can only tell that individual what you will tolerate. On the playground, the children will go all the way over to the fence to play, because they feel safe within the sense of boundaries. They understand where they're allowed to go, and they feel safe within those parameters.

Any parent knows that a big part of parenting is teaching your children where the boundaries are. The key is to have—and hold to—effective consequences. If you're setting boundaries with a teenage girl, the cell phone is a hugely powerful motivator. Tell her she won't have her phone for twenty-four hours. A boy? Take away his cell phone and video games for twenty-four hours. If your child's behavior doesn't change, then you don't have the right consequences. You need to find better, more effective consequences, or you need to escalate them. You want your children to feel and suffer the consequences of their decisions.

Of course, we could go on and on about parental boundaries, and those remain flexible because we are dealing with a child who is growing up. As your child grows, develops, and becomes capable of handling boundaries that are further and further removed from his or her parents, then the boundaries need to change.

The Exception

You've heard me say it like a beating drum: "With effective and consistent consequences, boundaries work." But, there is an exception, and I cannot finish this chapter without addressing the scenarios where boundaries are not enough.

When you are dealing with someone who has a personality disorder, an abusive or violent personality, or an addiction, or is suicidal, you cannot change the marriage by being intentional with your love. The individual may perceive your boundaries as an excuse to give up on the relationship, and this kind of behavior calls for greater support and direction than you can offer on your own. If he or she responds favorably to healthy boundaries, then you have a foundation to work with. But if not, you may have a problem bigger than boundaries can solve. In this situation, please seek professional help to guide you to a healthier place.

TOOL FOR THE JOURNEY:

With effective and consistent consequences, boundaries work.

Think about:

- Who has violated your boundaries in the past?

- With whom do you currently need to establish some boundaries?

- Is that person a bunny rabbit, a rattlesnake, or a mule? How rigid will your boundaries need to be?

Talk about:

- When do you feel I have violated your boundaries?

- How can I support you in your boundary setting?

- Are we going to do this? Will we establish this boundary?

o   This is an essential question to discuss. For
    example, if the husband's mom is causing
    problems by violating boundaries, then both
    husband and wife may need to set boundaries
    with the husband's mom, and you may both
    agree it is necessary, but the husband must be
    strong enough to know that he needs to be the
    face of the boundary setting. Remember to
    seek professional assistance for conversations
    and changes that feel emotionally dangerous,
    physically taxing, or bigger than what you can
    handle as a couple.

CHAPTER SIXTEEN

Inside the Mediation Room
Healthy Conflict and Resolution

I HATE COMPROMISE. I don't like that word at all. A lot of therapists and relational coaches will tell you that a healthy marriage is about the art of compromise, but I never want people to compromise. You see, compromise means I lose a point and you gain a point, and it always adds up to zero. It's a zero-sum game, a situation in which one person can win only by causing another person to lose. I don't want anybody's relationship to add up to zero! I want my relationship—and yours—to grow exponentially.

One definition of a compromise is "a change that makes something worse and is not done for a good reason."[6] (I don't know how it sounds to you, but that doesn't sound to me like a happy, healthy marriage.) With that definition, the opposite meaning is "to improve or enhance." (Sign me up for *that*, please.)

If we're going to avoid compromise, then we need to walk straight into healthy conflict and resolution. It's not easy; I know. But it's where the good stuff is hiding.

There's a scene in *Apollo 13* in which the astronauts are on their way back to earth. They've had to shut down all the navigational computers in the command module in order to save power, and it's time to bring it all back up. Because of the shutdown, the navigational computer doesn't know where they are. They have to take a sextant sighting to measure the angle between their module and Earth to locate where they are among the stars. The ship is rotating and bumping, but accuracy is essential. If they have the wrong measurement, they won't get home. Each of the astronauts has a separate and specific job which must be done precisely and in concert with one another. Truth be told, they each have their own physical and emotional distractions to deal with, but they have to set those aside to work on this one thing together. They must work as a team to locate the Earth, get the retroburn just right, and then they can each return to the multitude of other tasks of preparing the ship for reentry. If they fail to work well as a team, coordinating with one another, they won't get home. It is literally a matter of life or death.

Conflict in relationships has some similarities, since it often requires each person to set aside any distractions in order to focus on the pressing task at hand. Sometimes there is a sense of urgency, and a couple may need "all hands on deck" to handle a disagreement. In conflict resolution, you can only tackle one issue at a time. But too often, one person doesn't like where the conversation is going, so he or she tries to confuse the matter and bring up another issue or take them both down a rabbit trail. That kind of distraction isn't helpful, and it doesn't lead to resolution.

The Way That Doesn't Work

This may come as a shock to some readers, but the actual goal in a fight is not to win the argument. That's our culture's way of fighting: I want to win, and I need to win. Usually, the more invested a person is in holding on to the motivation to win, the more the conflict escalates and the more the couple separates.

There is a basic cycle to conflict that leads to separation, and these are the routines of an argument that lead nowhere good. See if you recognize any of these toxic steps in a destructive process:

1. **Insist that the issue is the most important thing.** Tell yourself that nothing is more important than winning this argument. If you start to falter or give in, remind yourself of this victory mantra. Winning is *everything.*
2. **Blindside the other person.** Make sure the other person is not ready to have this conversation with you at all.

It's especially helpful if that person is distracted or hungry. Jump right in with demands like, "We need to talk right now about what happened with Susie yesterday. We're talking about it now."

3. **Overwhelm the other person before he or she has thought it through.** Give the other person lots of one-sided perspectives and facts that you're absolutely sure of. When you do, you are communicating a subtext that says something like, "I've got all my arguments lined up, and I'm ready to annihilate you with my conclusions. Sure, you're defenseless, because you had no idea. You haven't thought it through. I don't care, though, because this increases my chances of winning."

4. **If logic isn't working, then just be hurtful.** The one who shoots the most arrows with the most accuracy is the winner. So, say things like, "You always do this. I knew you'd respond this way. You're just like your [mother, father, sister, etc.]."

5. **Forget the relationship.** Protect nothing but yourself. Winning is all that matters.

6. **If the other person continues to try to win, shoot more arrows.** Aim for his or her most sensitive and vulnerable areas. Return to old arguments, and if you begin to feel you're losing ground, bring up another topic of conflict to add to this one. Just keep piling them on. You're bound to win by majority.

7. **Repeat as necessary.**

Sound familiar? If you and your beloved have tried to resolve conflict this way, you're very normal. And you're likely frustrated, exhausted, and feeling that you're not only on separate pages, but reading from different books entirely.

A Better Way to Handle Conflict

There's a better way, a path of reconciliation, that leads to healing instead of separation. We need to recognize our wounds and our brokenness, so we can begin to see how they cause us to act in unloving, separating ways. When we are operating with that kind of humble spirit, then grace and mercy can flow into the conversation. We can choose to use words of connection rather than separation.

Let's look at the possibilities of this path instead.

1. **No issue is more important than the relationship, how well we love each other, and how we relate to one another.** Let's start with this foundational agreement that must always (*always*) be true. Read it again, please. Consider posting it on your refrigerator and your bathroom mirror and your nightstand. (I'm kidding. But then again, I'm not kidding at all. Do whatever it takes to keep this foundational.)

2. **Make an appointment to have conversations when you suspect an issue will lead to conflict.** When you make an appointment, you can approach the other person

and say, "Honey, we had an issue with Susie over the weekend, and I'd really like for us to sit down and talk about how we handled that individually and how we want to handle it moving forward. When would be a good time for us to discuss this?"

If the other person is wanting to be agreeable, or if he or she just wants to get it over with, that person might say, "Well, let's just talk about it right now." But don't fall into this trap. He or she is not prepared and has not thought it through as you have. You've presented an unfair and unbalanced situation. Instead, respond by saying, "I appreciate your heart for wanting to resolve this immediately, but I really want to allow time for you to think it through too. I've put a lot of thought into it since it happened, and I'd really like to give you that time as well. So, when is another time in the next day or two, or maybe next weekend, when we can sit down and talk about it after you've had a chance to think?"

This way, you're both prepared. You've engaged the prefrontal cortex, the part of your brain that plays a role in the regulation of complex behavior, thought, and functions. You've distanced yourselves from all the emotional reactivity that occurred when Susie was acting out, and you've had time to think rationally. You've set yourselves up for success to listen and to hear one another.

3. **Recognize when you are in danger of harming the relationship. And then stop.** Both of you need to agree that either person can choose to stop any conversation on any topic at any time, whenever he or she feels that either person is coming close to harming the relationship. Together you need to be committed and learn to stop doing harm, and that means stepping away—but you've got to stop in a very specific way. A lot of couples are really good at getting in a fight over something, and when it gets bad enough, they separate into their separate corners, stay silent for a few days, and wait for the storm to blow over. Then they'll sweep it under the rug, come back together to kiss and make up, but they haven't resolved the underlying issue. You must pause in a very specific, intentional way.

4. **Stop immediately.** That means that nobody takes a last-word potshot at the other person. Agree to stop, and here's the crucial point: together set the day and time to begin again. You can do this by saying, "We need to stop. It feels to me like we (not you, not me, but *we*) are harming the relationship, so I want to disengage from this conversation right now. I want to reengage with you about this topic," and then you set a specific time and day together, preferably within twenty-four hours, depending on schedules.

5. **When you reconnect, engage on an emotional level first.** Though it may be tempting to pick up where you left

off, don't talk about the issue right away. In too many cases, the couple will go to their individual corners without agreeing about what was happening between them—they just sort of abandon the fight without clear communication. They go to their separate corners to nurse their wounds, and perhaps it comes up again a few days later. Then, like a pair of boxers who stopped mid-swing, they take their stance again, both of them ready to follow through and complete that swing. Almost instantaneously, they're back in the same exact emotional state they were in before. Why? Because they don't know how the subject escalated in the first place. They don't know how they got to that emotional place, so they simply return to it.

Instead, when you come back together, start by engaging emotionally. Begin with a simple series of questions. "Honey, what did I say or do that caused you to pull away from me? What caused you to feel like I was pulling away from you? What did I say that triggered you?" Once you've answered it from one person's perspective, then trade places and let the other person ask as well. Check each other's emotional pulse and well-being before going back to the topic at hand. (This is similar to how every NFL football team looks at game film. This kind of analysis is an essential part of getting ready for the next game.) Then affirm one another.

6. **Discuss the issue.** Now that you've engaged and connected on an emotional level, and once you've

discovered the triggers, you can reengage the issue. The actual task of finding a solution isn't all that difficult when you're connected emotionally. When you have heart attitudes in the right place, when you each want to understand the other person's perspective, and when you are each committed to finding the answer that works for both of you, then you can truly solve problems together. No issue or challenge can divide you.

7. **Repeat as necessary.** If you come back together and you can't connect emotionally, stop again. Do no harm. Stop immediately and set another time to reconnect. Why? Because no issue is more important than how you are relating to one another.

There really is a better way. Picture a rubber band, one that is strong and tight. When we are in relational struggle, we are stretching and weakening the bonds of the relationship, just like a rubber band that gets stretched too far. Once it's out of shape, it's hard to rebuild that elasticity. That's not what I want for you, and I know it's not what you want for you. Instead, strive to move closer and tighter to one another. Never allow anything to cause the bonds of the relationship to stretch and weaken. Stay close, tight, and together.

TOOL FOR THE JOURNEY:

We need to recognize our wounds and our brokenness, so we can begin to see how they cause us to act in unloving, separating ways. When we are operating with that kind of humble spirit, then grace and mercy can flow into the conversation.
We can choose a path of reconciliation that leads to healing instead of separation.

Think about:

- In your conflicts, have you found yourself chasing bunny trails and feeling as if the two of you never get anything resolved? How does that make you feel about the relationship?

- In your conflicts, has your goal been to "win" and to get what you want, or has your goal been to resolve the issue?

- As you look at the steps in the destructive process, how many of them do you recognize as part of the conflict process in your relationship?

- Remember one of the founding principles of intentional love: *No issue is more important than the relationship, how well we love each other, and how we relate to one another.* What would be the impact on you, your beloved, and your relationship together, if you were able to engage one another based on this principle? What would that look like? How would you engage differently, based on this principle?

- Think about how your relationship could improve if both of you agreed to stop the fight whenever either person felt the relationship was being harmed. Imagine how it could be better if you set a new time and day to revisit the issue. Would this be difficult for you?

- If you follow this principle, instead of jumping right back into the place where the two of you were when you stopped fighting, could you take time to understand what went wrong the last time and affirm your commitment to each other and the relationship?

Talk about:

- Discuss the destructive ways you recognized that the two of you have been handling conflict.

- Recognize together whether you have been focused on "winning" and getting what you want rather than finding the answer that works for both parties.

- Talk about how you feel about the foundational principle: *No issue is more important than the relationship, how well we love each other, and how we relate to one another.* What can this look like in your marriage?

- ○ How would you act differently in the midst of conflict?

- ○ How could you be held accountable to this principle?

- ○ Can you commit to using this principle?

- Talk about how you feel about the principle of stopping immediately, any time you sense one or both of you is doing harm to the relationship.

  - ○ How would you act differently in the midst of conflict?

  - ○ How could you be held accountable to this principle?

  - ○ Can you commit to using this principle?

- Share how you feel about engaging emotionally before reengaging about the issue.

  - ○ How would you act differently in the midst of conflict?

  - ○ How could you be held accountable to this principle?

  - ○ Can you commit to using this principle?

CHAPTER SEVENTEEN

Where You Really Want to Go for Dinner

How to Pursue Vulnerability

"I'M GETTING HUNGRY. WHERE should we have dinner tonight?"

"I don't know. What sounds good to you?"

"I can't decide. What do you want?"

"Oh, I don't know."

Does this sound familiar? It happens any night of the week in relationships all across America. Somehow, we become paralyzed by indecision when it's time to eat dinner.

The truth of the matter is that there's usually something hiding behind the "I don't know" of the dinner debate. The husband may feel, after the week he's had, that he has earned a nice, big, juicy piece of meat with a side of buttered bread and potatoes. The wife may feel that she'd like to have a light dinner with salad, soup, and zero carbs. Or, the roles may be reversed: he's feeling like an herbivore while she's carnivorous.

It doesn't seem as though this conversation should be a vulnerable one, but somehow this daily topic gets tricky for a lot of couples. For a myriad of reasons, they're not saying what they really want or why they really want it, and there are many other factors in play that they're not talking about. Either one of them may feel like eating their feelings (i.e., too many calories of comfort food) or starving themselves. One may want to overindulge while the other may want to watch calories. It may seem simple and obvious, but when they bring those topics to the table, they can begin down a path of openness and honesty. With practice, we can learn how to talk more openly and intimately, from dinner choices to difficult emotions.

Five Levels of Communication[7]

As a society, we have some cultural understandings of what is appropriate for conversation upon first meeting someone. Most people, at least those with a degree of emotional intelligence and social awareness, do not begin with the deep intimacies of their lives upon first introduction. There's a reason for that: it's weird. We have a sort of conversational hopscotch that we play as we advance forward in a relationship with someone, whether it's your coffee barista or your sister's new boyfriend at the Thanksgiving table.

First, we begin with clichés. This is the most basic, shallow level of communication. These are the rituals and the questions we ask when we're passing someone in the hallway or sharing an elevator with a stranger. "How are you?" "Fine, you?" "Nice weather we're having, isn't it?" "How 'bout them Broncos?" You offer nothing personal, and you expect nothing personal. These are programmed greetings that we exchange with people we expect we'll never see again. You're simply acknowledging your awareness of another human being. It fosters a sense of safety and well-being, because nobody has really offered anything at all.

The next step involves sharing information. This is likely the conversational place where you interact with your coworkers, and it's what we generally call "small talk." These conversations consist of facts and figures, dates and times, appointments, and logistics. There is slightly more risk involved, since you could give the wrong information, but that's still a common error and not a personal failure. These exchanges are basic and minimal, and they change from day to day, but they're to be expected for most interactions in our lives. Sadly, some marriages stay at this basic level. As couples manage their finances, menus, chores, and calendars, they may stay in this emotional no-man's land, where no vulnerability is required of either person. It's a functional place, but not a place of intimacy.

As we go deeper into relationship, the third level is where we begin sharing ideas and opinions. We begin to share what we're thinking, to ask what's on the other person's mind. This level pulls back the curtain a bit, because when you offer your thought, opinion, or idea, you give the other person something to disagree with. Remember that question, "Where should we have dinner tonight?" It falls into this category. If you can't tell your spouse where you want to go for dinner, then you likely cannot progress to any deeper levels of communication. But this is the space where you get to know someone, how they think, what they prefer, what they enjoy and dislike. It's where relationships begin to form and take root.

The fourth level is where things start to get scary, because it's where we begin to share values and feelings. We share our hopes, dreams, values, aspirations, and these are intimate pieces of information. When you share these with someone, when that someone knows what is most important to you, he or she now has leverage to use against you. But on the positive side, this level of communication also lets the other person see who you truly are. When your spouse notices that you're upset, you are stepping into this level as you explain what's really on your mind. When you say, "I love you" in a meaningful way, not perfunctorily, you're in this fourth level of communication. You've shared your feelings, and you've invited the other person closer.

The fifth and deepest level of conversation is where we share intimacy, deep insights, needs, and confessions with one another. This is the component that builds a truly dynamic marriage. When we can share what we've done wrong, when we can offer a genuine apology and forgiveness to one another, when we can share how we feel about the other person, and when we can talk openly about what we need—this is where we truly take risks together. These are the moments that can feel embarrassing or threatening, so we tend to avoid them. But this is where genuine intimacy hides, like a box waiting to be opened.

When you find yourself struggling to communicate effectively, take a look at the level on which the two of you are communicating. Are you stuck on a more superficial level, avoiding a deeper conversation? Has one of you attempted to go deeper without building the necessary foundation? Are there certain levels that you seem to always avoid together? Think about how you can shift the conversation to a level that's safe for both of you.

Strong Personalities Go Second

I have a strong personality, and I know I have a tendency to bowl over the person in front of me. It took me a while to learn that I needed to seek Cindy's opinion before I gave my own. I almost never tell her what I want without first asking what she would like. So, in the great dinner debates, I just keep turning it back to her, asking her to decide first.

Finally, she rebelled. "Why do I always have to go first?"

"Honey, it's because I know that if I voice my opinion first, you're very inclined to just go along with it and I'll never get to hear your true feelings. If you go first, then I will still tell you what I think, and we can join together in the decision-making process."

You see, when Cindy and I first got married, I bought into the idea of the husband being in charge. I thought that if we couldn't reach consensus together, then I'd just have to make the decision. I know now that was hogwash. Anytime I was left to make the decision to break the tie, well, let's just say the best decision didn't get made. I learned the hard way that I don't want to make all the decisions in our family. It's not good for either of us. I don't want all the power, and I don't want Cindy always acquiescing. I want to strive to listen as an equal, to give us both an equal voice so that we can make the best possible decisions together.

If you know you have the stronger personality, then make a conscious choice. Don't state your opinion before you hear what your spouse has in mind. **Listen first; listen second; listen last.**

On to Bigger Decisions

For a lot of people, it's difficult to share emotions openly and honestly. That's a very vulnerable place, and if we can't share our thoughts about where we want to eat, then we can't talk about anything else. I know it's a simple thing, deciding where we'll have dinner, but I also know that it can set the tone for other decisions.

If you start with something easy, it will grow into bigger things. Imagine being able to talk about the deepest questions of your heart. When you can talk openly about what you want for dinner, then you have started down a path where nothing is off-limits.

Unless the house is on fire, there are virtually no decisions that have to be made right now. Every decision will wait until you can come to a place of agreement and with an answer that works for both of you. Slow down and listen. And if you're the dominant personality, then listen even more.

TOOL FOR THE JOURNEY:

Listen first; listen second; listen last.

Think about:

- When have you used each of the five levels of communication?

- Do you feel you're getting enough of a voice in the relationship?

Talk about:

- Set a recurring weekly time to meet together outside of your home. Use this time to connect about the schedule for the coming week, but then go deeper and discuss how the relationship is going. Ask the following questions:

o   How do you feel our relationship is going?

o   What's working well for you in our relationship?

o   What areas need improvement?

o   Do I help you to feel heard?

o   Am I doing things that make you feel good about who you are?

o   Am I causing you to pull away from me?

o   What is it like to disagree with me?

CHAPTER EIGHTEEN

More Than "I'm Sorry"
How to Reconcile

"TELL YOUR SISTER YOU'RE sorry," parents say to their preschoolers.

"I don't want to," says the little brother.

"Tell her you're sorry," they repeat, threatening to take away a toy, a reward, a visit to the park, or some screen time.

"I'm sorry," he says with a furrowed brow and no heart connection.

Now to the sister, "Tell your brother you forgive him."

"I forgive you," she says, having no idea what it means.

That's what we teach our children. I can tell you that I never learned confession and forgiveness as a process to resolve true hurt in my childhood. There were lots of battles between my two sisters and me, and that made for a lot of conflict. I don't remember learning how to confess what I had done wrong, and I don't remember hearing my sisters confess to me what they had done wrong. Forgiveness was certainly not something I grew up knowing how to do. I never learned what it was really about. I found these practices in my adult life, and I had to chase them down as a matter of necessity and healing.

A few chapters ago, I told you about two couples in high conflict: Dan and Julie, and Rick and Rhonda. In both marriages, the men had had affairs, and the wives held on to the memory like a weapon to use as needed. Anytime one of the wives felt that she was losing an argument, she'd beat her husband over the head with old memories. These couples came to me on the brink of divorce, and I coached them through sincere confessions and forgiveness. Both couples have since moved forward in their marriages, they've experienced new milestones and crises, and each of them have been in touch to tell me they continue to rate their marriages as a 9 on a thriving scale of 1 to 10.

Let me talk you through this process, just as I would if you were seated in my office.

How to Apologize: Seven Steps

You may use these notes to help you identify the steps in the process, but please use your own words. That's where everything hinges: on your own heart's response. Turn to your spouse, hold hands, and make a lot of eye contact. Here we go. You can do this, because no issue is more important than the way you're relating to one another.

Seven Steps of Confession:[8]

1. **Address everyone involved.**

    Bring together everyone who is affected by the
    wrongful actions. If it's just you as a couple, then this
    conversation is just between you and your beloved.
    If children are aware of the transgression, then it
    is healthy to include them in your apology as well.
    Apologizing to children is sometimes more difficult,
    but certainly as important.

2. **Avoid *if, but,* and *maybe.***

    Do not try to make excuses. Do not try to justify
    what you did. You can't say, "I'm sorry I yelled at
    you, but maybe if you had had the directions ready,
    I wouldn't have needed to shout." No, just apologize.

3. **Admit specifically.**

    Our actions always flow out of our heart attitudes,
    so it's important to specifically name the attitudes
    and actions involved. You must develop a heart
    attitude that says you take responsibility for your
    own brokenness, and that you will no longer allow
    it to drive your behavior. You might say, "I hurt you
    when I yelled at you, and I felt [thought] it was okay
    because you got in the way of what I wanted. It made
    me feel bigger to watch you feel smaller. I know that
    attitude is wrong."

4. **Acknowledge the hurt.**

   Show your awareness that your actions were damaging. You can say, "I understand now that I hurt you with my words and actions."

5. **Accept the consequences.**

   Offer to make restitution. Tell your beloved that you are willing to do what it takes to restore your relationship. If this incident involved violation of trust, then tell your partner you are willing to be open and transparent in whatever way they need in order to restore that trust.

6. **Alter your behavior.**

   Tell the other person the change you intend to make. Say what you will do differently next time this trigger or a similar one occurs, such as, "I don't want to hurt you in this way again. I know I belittled you and caused you to feel smaller and less than who you really are. I know I harmed your sense of self-worth. I am going to work on being aware of when that attitude appears as well as what triggers it. In the future, I will not raise my voice to you, even if I am in a hurry. This will help me to not respond with the attitude that it is okay to treat you that way." Because you have identified the heart attitude, the action will be easier to change, and you will increase trust.

7. **Ask for forgiveness.**

Sincerely look at your spouse and ask, "Will you forgive me?" Do not presume that forgiveness is your entitled guarantee. With these seven steps, you've done your part, and now it is up to your beloved to respond.

These steps seem lengthy and complex, but with practice, you can say it all in one good paragraph. It could look like this: "I understand that I yelled at you, and I was demeaning to you. I can see now that the reason I yelled at you is because there's a part of me that wants to displace my pain onto you. I'm going to change this about myself, and I will control my actions. I commit to you that I never want to demean you again. I need to do some work to look at my attitude, to determine what made me think it's okay for me to displace my pain onto you. Will you please forgive me?"

Want another example? Go back to chapter 10, in the apologies between the two couples. In these examples, all seven steps fit together in one short paragraph. You'll see this really is a lot easier than it sounds. Now you've opened the door for true forgiveness to happen.

How to Forgive: Four Promises

When your partner has finished apologizing, it is your turn to respond with these four promises. Yes, ultimately the goal is to have your partner share enough understanding and/or show enough change in behavior and attitude so you can freely give these promises from your heart, but for now, you can make all four, none, one or two, and you can make them in any order.

These promises don't mean you're going to be perfect any more than the other person will be perfect in their actions either. But if you're going to speak them, the promises have to come from your heart. Often, forgiveness must be granted before it can be felt, so you will probably need to step into the waters of granting forgiveness before you begin to feel peace in your spirit. But that peace will come eventually when you open your hands and let go of this offense done to you.

If you were sitting in my office, now that one of you has finished apologizing, I would then turn to the other one of you and ask, "How do you want to respond?" Now, hear me on this: *You are not required to give all or any of the promises of forgiveness. It doesn't matter how many promises you make at this stage.* You can begin with one promise, and simply start there.

Four Promises of Forgiveness:[9]

1. **I promise I will not dwell on this incident.**

   I don't believe we have control over every single thought that comes into our heads, but I do believe we have control over those on which we choose to dwell. We can be in charge of what we choose to continue to think about, and if we are honest with one another, sometimes we carry out elaborate plans of revenge in our imaginations. Thoughts are a kind of fuel for our feelings, and when you stop thinking about a wrong done to you, the anger subsides. With these words, you promise to stop feeding the monster of resentment by choosing not to dwell on it anymore.

2. **I promise I will not bring this incident up and use it against you.**
   This promise says you will put this memory away, and you will no longer hold on to it as a weapon for your protection or defense. After this, you won't bring it up anymore.

3. **I promise I will not talk to others about this incident.**
   This is a pretty good principle to live by, since involving other people generally complicates and wounds the relationship. With these words, you are saying, "I won't go get my army, while you get your army, so that the one with the biggest army wins the argument." You won't tell your officemate, your mother, your best friend, your beer buddy, or the classmates at your college reunion. This doesn't mean you won't discuss it in a professional setting if necessary. I think we all need mentors and confidants who can speak with objectivity and wisdom into our

lives. But many people seek accomplices rather than true friends or mentors. With these words, you are promising you won't involve other people as a tool to complicate the wound and the relationship.

4. **I promise I will not allow this incident to stand between us or hinder our personal relationship.**
   I think this promise is the hardest one, but it's perhaps the most important one. When you make this promise, you're committing to choose to draw close once again. That's the whole point: to connect again and stay connected. This can feel like a most vulnerable place to be, because you are laying down your defenses and needing to trust that the other person is going to fulfill what they said in their apology. But we have to choose to draw close once again. In choosing to practice confession and forgiveness, you develop a trust, a depth, and a breadth to your love that cannot be created in any other way.

Often, when we talk about forgiveness, a natural question emerges: *"What if they do it again?"* It's a fair question, and it deserves an answer. When there is a repeat offender, then we have to be more careful with confession, and we must make sure that the offender truly understands the attitude behind his or her actions. When a person's heart has changed, that individual's actions will change as well. If he or she continues to be hurtful, then we must look more closely at the offender's heart to make sure that person understands the wounds he or she is inflicting. The bottom line is, if the repeat offender does it again, then he or she will have the opportunity to confess his or her sin once again, and you'll have the chance once again to forgive.

If you cannot say all four promises—or even one, then we can talk about what needs to be done to get you to that place. If you don't know, then you need to commit to your partner that you will be intentional about thinking it through and seeking to understand what is still getting in the way. As part of that commitment, set a time when you will get back to them. Even then, you may not have all the answers, but it is essential to keep your commitment by getting together when you said you would and then sharing what you have been thinking and feeling.

Each of these commitments (to work on understanding your heart, and to get together again) is deeply important because your partner is hanging in a very vulnerable place. Your beloved has just come out from his or her protective castle, crossed the moat, laid down all weapons, and confessed his or her weakness (wounds and brokenness). Nothing feels quite so vulnerable as this, and it is as if your partner's heart is laid open before the one person who has the greatest ability to slice and dice it. Your partner needs to know that you will meet him or her with the same vulnerability. These promises and commitments are the fertile ground for forgiveness and healing.

TOOL FOR THE JOURNEY:

**The steps of confession and the promises of forgiveness
are the glue that keep you and your beloved together.
When a person's heart has changed,
his or her behavior will change as well.**

Think about:

- What emotions rise up when you consider doing the seven A's of confession? Does it feel too complicated? Scary? Too vulnerable?

- On your own, mentally wrestle with the statement, "You must develop a heart attitude that says you take responsibility for your own brokenness and that you will no longer allow it to drive your behavior." It is a struggle to get at the underlying attitude that says it is okay to treat my beloved as less than. This is the hardest part.

- Remember a problematic episode or event in the history of your relationship:

o   What did you do that was destructive to the relationship? How did you hurt your beloved?

o   What attitude allowed you to think it was okay for you to act this way, even if you only thought it was appropriate for that instant? Were you being selfish, like the Cookie Monster? Was your ego saying that you and your feelings are more important than your beloved's? Were you being self-righteous? Were you convinced you were the only one who knew "the truth"?

o   If you are still struggling with getting at the underlying attitude, then after both of you have calmed down and can be rational with each other again, ask your beloved to tell you what he or she felt and thought at the time.

• In your mind, go through each of the seven steps. Formulate how you would address each one. Make some notes.

• What emotions rise up when you think about making the Four Promises of Forgiveness? Do you not feel ready? Maybe you don't want to, or you don't think you can do it. Maybe you just don't feel like forgiving.

• Forgiveness starts as a mental process—not an emotional process. Logically think through the meaning of the four promises.

Talk about:

- For Confession: Make an appointment with your beloved and let him or her know the purpose of your appointment.

  o   Arrange seating so you are looking directly at each other.

  o   Hold one of your partner's hands. (Your other hand will have your notes you've prepared.)

  o   Look your partner in the eye—*a lot*. Definitely make eye contact as you say each sentence.

  o   Go through your seven steps, verbally.

  o   Start breathing again, and congratulations. You have just accomplished one of the most important acts of intentional love that will move your relationship into the thriving relationship category!

- For Forgiveness:

  o   Listen to your beloved with an open but discerning mind.

  o   Get your resistance out of the way. Don't let yourself think a statement that begins with "I don't."

o   Seek to discern your partner's heart: Is he or she sincere? Is your partner accepting full responsibility for his or her actions? Does your partner have a new understanding of his or her underlying attitude?

o   When your partner is finished, take some time to absorb not just the words but the his or her heart and intentions.

o   Search your heart: Did your partner touch your heart in a deep place? Are you able to let go of what you have been grasping that has been protecting your heart?

o   Consider the promises one at a time, in whatever order you want. Ask yourself: Am I able to freely and sincerely offer this promise from my heart?

o   Make eye contact.

o   For each one that you feel you can say, begin with "I promise," and then state the promise.

o   If there are any of the promises that you cannot sincerely and freely give, tell your beloved why you cannot make these promises and discuss what else you need in order to let go of the fear. Do you feel there is a problematic episode or event in the history of your relationship that needs to be dealt with? Is that what's keeping you from feeling or showing how much you love your partner? Be honest with yourself and your beloved and decide if you need to set another time to discuss it further.

CHAPTER NINETEEN

You Are Safe Here
Learn to Heal

JOHN MAXWELL IS AN author, speaker, and pastor, and he's one of the world's gurus on the topics of leadership and living a life of significance. In his book *The 21 Irrefutable Laws of Leadership*,[10] Maxwell's first law is called the Law of the Lid. Essentially, he explains that a person's leadership ability is determined by his or her level of effectiveness, and if you are a 7 on the leadership scale, then in most cases you won't be able to lead someone who is an 8, 9, or 10. You cannot lead someone to a level higher than your own. I believe the same is true in terms of how we love another person. If I love myself at a level 5, I cannot love Cindy better than a level 4. If I aim to love my wife better, then I need to begin by learning to love myself better.

In the introduction to this book, we talked about the three-legged stool. A balanced life of love calls me to learn to love God with everything I've got, love myself with everything I've got, and love others with everything I've got. Without any one of these, the stool falls over. If you don't love yourself well—the hardest one for us to do—then your stool falls over. If you truly desire to love your significant other better, then you have to commit to being intentional about learning to love yourself better. Part of this process is learning that when your wounds are causing you to feel you have to have certain things, these feelings are not accurate. This allows you to stop grasping for those things and instead focus on caring for and serving the other person in your life, you learn to love yourself as well as the other person.

What Is Self-Love?

Part of getting in touch with your own woundedness and brokenness involves learning how to love yourself better. Self-love can begin with one small step: learn how to accept a compliment. In our culture, it is not politically correct to receive a compliment, so we have learned to deflect anything positive that someone says to us and about us. Picture this: You've put together a weekend seminar, and someone comes up to you after the last session to say, "You did such a great job! That was incredible! Look at all the notes I took—you've changed my life with this information. What a gift to my life. Thank you so much!"

Most people in this situation wouldn't know what to do or how to respond. It seems like the correct answer is to say, "Oh, no, it was nothing. It was my team." Or

"It was all God." Hogwash! Somebody had to have the organizational skills to put it all together and deliver the material. Yes, you may believe God did it, but He used *you*. He gave the opportunity and gifts to *you*. He gave you the gifts of organization and communication, and He asked you to obey him by serving and leading this way. The right answer is to own this giftedness so you can send all the glory to Him.

With that in mind, a better answer is, "Thank you so much. I feel very thankful and blessed to use the gifts of organization God has given me so that He could change the lives of the people here." Do you see the difference? You can own your part *and* give glory to the One who gave you the ability. We have to learn how to love ourselves in order to receive compliments. When we do, then we open the gates to giving meaningful compliments and deeper input to others, which is loving them at a higher level.

I've told you a little bit about the winding path that brought me out of corporate America, delayed my retirement, and landed me on a career path as a therapist and marriage counselor. So yes, you know I was not planning on becoming a counselor. The truth is that I was a psych major for three years in college—not because I cared about psychology at that point in my life, but because the classes were easy. But I jumped ship and went into business. Thirty years later, God touched me on the shoulder and whispered, "Remember that psych thing? I was serious about that. I want you to go to seminary." He gave me the skills, ability, and giftedness. If I am blessing people, if people are learning anything from me, then that is not just from me. It is God working through me. Part of self-love is learning what our gifting is, what our passions are, and being able to acknowledge and receive those compliments.

Open the Doors of Your Heart

Robert Boyd Munger was a Presbyterian pastor in Berkeley, California, in the 1950s and '60s, and he wrote a timeless sermon that is so powerful that it's still making the rounds in Christian circles fifty years later. His sermon and subsequent pamphlet was titled *My Heart, Christ's Home*,[11] and in it he explored a metaphor of the rooms in a house. Each room represented a different part of our lives. Here's the gist of the sermon:

The owner of the house invites Jesus into the various rooms of the house. He tells Jesus he has shown them all there is, but Jesus says, "Well, there is one more room in this house."

"No, Jesus, I've let you into every room."

Jesus sniffs the pungent air. He says, "No, something doesn't smell quite right. Something needs to be cleaned out." They go upstairs and they find a closet door. Jesus points to the door, and he says, "It's in there."

The guy stands in front of the door, blocking the way, barring Jesus from going in. He has padlocked and chained the door. "No, Jesus," he says. "This has nothing to do with you."

Jesus won't force his way in. He says, "Well, if you won't let Me into that room, then I cannot stay in this house. I cannot stay here with that smell throughout the house." Finally, the man steps aside and lets Jesus in, and Jesus begins to clean out the mess.

We are just like the man in this story, aren't we? That's why we have our emotional barriers in place—to hide our dark sides from ourselves. But there is also a spiritual barrier, which we hold in place to deceive ourselves into thinking we are hiding the darkness from God as well. We all have that barrier, where we try to keep Christ away from that dark closet. I don't want my beloved or my Lord anywhere near that dark closet. I don't even want to go there myself. I'm ashamed and embarrassed about those secrets, and I work hard to cover it up and keep it from getting exposed. We protect ourselves from other people, but sometimes we protect ourselves from our own truth as well.

Part of self-love is coming face to face with the reality that, like everyone else, you are wounded and broken and incapable of loving yourself or others perfectly. In other words, you too have a closet that smells bad, just like everyone else, and you need to clean it out. You will need to work on forgiving yourself for much of what is in your closet.

Revealing the Monster Under the Bed

Do you remember when you were five years old, and you woke up in the middle of the night needing to go to the bathroom? You had to go, but you were afraid to stick your foot off the side because somehow you got it in your head that there was a monster under the bed. There was no way you would put even one finger over the edge. You knew the monster would get it. So, you called for Mommy or Daddy. As soon as your mom or dad turned on the light, what happened to the monster? Poof! It was gone. It had no power.

Some of the yuck (this is a highly technical counseling term that you may not fully understand but suffice it to say it means your wounds) is like the proverbial monster under the bed. This is what happens with some of your wounds once they are brought into the light of day, where they can be named and examined. They lose their power, and they have no control over you. Remember when I learned that I had let Cindy down by not giving her my full attention at the end of the day? The hurt seemed insurmountable and too scary to talk about until we brought it out into the light of day with our counselor. The conflict lost its power and has no control over us anymore.

Other wounds in your closet are deeper. These wounds come out of the trauma you may have experienced, or they may be the result of physical, emotional, or sexual abuse that was done to you. These wounds will never be completely healed. If you have suffered these kinds of wounds, please seek out professional help to uncover and examine them in a controlled environment and using a safe process. Your partner can help with the healing process by being patient, reliable, empathetic, and striving to understand the emotional pain. He or she can also be an integral part of the healing process as the two of you learn how to manage those wounds and determine what triggers them. It is possible to get to the place where you are managing the wounds instead of the wounds managing you and your life.

Learning to Heal the Other Person

We are attracted to people because of the way they look, think, and act, but as I've said before, I think there's something much deeper going on. I believe God is at work at a deeper level, and He allows us to be drawn to and attracted to people based on our wounds. It's not that we are attracted to each other's wounds, but rather that our own woundedness and brokenness will trigger the other person's, and vice versa. *When our wounds are brought into the light, they can be healed or managed. I believe we are meant to trigger one another's wounds so they may be healed or managed.*

Christians have a fancy word for this: sanctification. It's a big word that means becoming set apart, free from impurities, more like Christ. I believe that one of the roles God has for me as Cindy's spouse is to be one of the tools of her sanctification; she does the same for me. Together, we reveal each other's wounds so that together we may bring them into the light. It's very difficult to see your own wounds clearly, but it's easier to see another person's. In marriage, we can see each other better than we can see ourselves, and this kind of clarity brings healing. I do this for Cindy, and I need her to do the same for me.

In the Christian faith, when a person receives salvation, a pastor will ask, "Do you accept Jesus Christ as your Lord and Savior?" When my pastor asked me this question, I said yes, but I don't think I really knew what I was saying. I understood what that question meant, but I didn't know how to give Him that role in my life. Thirty years later, I still struggle with allowing Christ to be the Lord of my life. There are parts of my life that He is not Lord of at all. I'm not proud of this, but it is true. I'm a fallen, sinful being, incapable of loving myself, my God, or anyone else perfectly. I am forever learning how to make him Lord of my life, how to allow love to be the dominant thing that guides my actions and my behaviors, and how to love my wife in ways that help her become the woman God created her to be. It is a journey of learning that will last for as long as I live on this earth.

For all of my days, I am on a mission to learn how to *love better sooner.*

TOOL FOR THE JOURNEY:

**On a level we aren't aware of, we are attracted
to people who trigger our wounds.
When our wounds are brought into the light,
they can be healed or managed. I believe we are meant to
trigger one another's wounds so they may heal
or be managed.**

Think about:

- Many people, particularly women, were raised with the idea that they needed to be focused on others and not worry about taking care of themselves. Are you in this category?

- What emotions does this chapter stimulate in you?

- Do you find it confusing? upsetting? or freeing? affirming?

- Consider and identify your feelings about being

    o   wounded by significant others

    o   broken by people in positions of trust and/or authority

- Are you able to at least begin to see you are no more broken or wounded than any other?

- Are you able to acknowledge and know in your heart you are just as valuable as any other? That you are just as worthy as anyone else?

- Have you identified wounds and brokenness in you?

- Can you distinguish between the "monster under the bed" and the deeper wounds? Have you experienced the relief of shining a light toward the monster under the bed when those wounds are no longer a problem?

- Have you seen that the deeper wounds can be managed even if not completely healed?

- Consider this statement: "If you truly desire to love your significant other better, then you have to commit to being intentional about loving yourself." Do you agree or disagree?

- Consider this statement: "When you let go of what you feel you need most, and when you focus on caring for and serving the other person in your life, you learn to love yourself as well as the other person." This refers to unhealthy neediness. Everyone needs to have healthy boundaries around them, and we each need the freedom to not allow others to have the power to violate those boundaries. Love can only grow in an environment where you feel safe.

Talk about:

- As your partner, how can I help heal you?

- What exacerbates your wounds?

- What is soothing/healing to you?

- How can I love you better?

CHAPTER TWENTY

The Power to Choose

Love Better Sooner

THE JOURNEY OF *APOLLO 13* was a life-or-death situation, and that's where the metaphor breaks down. In a marriage, the consequences are not so dire, and the risks are not so high. But there are consequences to your daily decisions, actions, and reactions—both intentional and otherwise—that can cause your relationship to flourish or fail. While these are not life or death, they deeply affect the *life of your love*.

It's easy to love the other person when he or she is acting in lovable ways. But love gets far more difficult when the other person is acting in ways that feel unlovable, unapproachable, and even downright hurtful. In other words, when that person is being driven unconsciously by his or her wounds. That is where love gets hard. It is where love becomes a decision.

You have a choice every single day. You can choose how you will talk to your beloved, what tone of voice and which word choices you will use. You can choose to pour a cup of coffee to your partner's liking while you pour your own. You can choose to listen first and last and in between. You have the choice to confess or apologize, to openly acknowledge the ways you were wrong. You have the choice to forgive—both your beloved and yourself. You can choose vulnerability in ways great and small, to walk into the hard conversations. You can choose to manage your wounds, to not let them own you. You have a choice every single day. You have a choice *right now.* Your chance is never not now. Your chance to choose is right now.

Imagine you're driving home from a long trip, and you've come to an intersection on a country road. You are faced with two different paths—one to your right, and one to your left. On your left is the entrance to a superhighway, and on your right is a winding road down into a dark valley. The superhighway is the path you've always taken, and you know that route without really having to think about it. The signs are clear, you've traveled it a thousand times, and you can hop on it again and know exactly where it goes. This superhighway is like the fear-based path you've always chosen with your beloved. When emotions rise, you have the path you've always taken. You know your partner's cues and signs, you know which areas escalate quickly, and you can manipulate the path pretty well. It is easy to protect yourself. You could write that script because you know where that road ends. It may be driven by fear, but at least it's familiar and it feels safe.

Or you can choose a new path. The road on the right looks dark and unknown, and you're going to have to slow down since you haven't gone this way before. It's uncharted territory. There are ruts, potholes, and some low branches that might scrape your car. You may have to go through the mud, and you might get stuck—you may even need to call for some professional help if you can't navigate it on your own. This journey will call for you to put a lot of trust in your partner. But in the end, this path leads to a far better destination, the place you really want to be together. When we cultivate trust, then we can increase our peace, which builds contentment, and these ultimately produce joy.

This is where the rubber meets the road. The highway is easy, but it's based on lies, distortion, and fear. The bumpy path is more difficult, and it calls you to self-awareness, humility, trust, and truth. The decision to go down the unknown path is a choice empowered by your ability to lean into the five intentional practices of love: service and sacrifice, delight, healing, vulnerability, and forgiveness. You have a choice: to do what you've always done, or to love better sooner.

The Pleasure Is Mine

In scenes of *Apollo 13*, there comes a moment when the astronauts can do no more. The crew has followed all of the instructions. They've done everything they can do to prepare. They brace themselves for their reentry, intensely aware that this is the crucial moment. It gives me chills every time.

I feel that same sense of anticipation as we finish these final moments together. I feel as if I am setting you free for the final stretch home. We've done all the legwork. I don't know how this will go for you and your beloved, but that's up to the two of you now. I do know this: I believe in people and therefore in you, I remain ready to partner with you, and I know you have what it takes to love well.

What can this look like? You can choose once again to delight in each other, just as you did in the beginning of your relationship. Wonder and wonderfulness can permeate your lives, both individually and together. You may stop thinking in terms of conflicts and fighting, and instead, you may find yourself running to your beloved, knowing he or she is a safe place for you. You may want to tear down the walls that separate you, and you'll feel safe to reveal the sounds and brokenness that keep you from loving one another well. You'll no longer bring weapons to your arguments, but rather, you will lay down your armor and engage the topic together. It's possible that you will no longer have issues over sex, since you will become consumed with creating love—not just in the bedroom, but throughout the intimate interactions of your daily lives.

I foresee homes filled with a joyful love born out of peace and contentment, fueled by a total willingness and desire to sacrifice and serve, to delight and heal, to join with your beloved in the union of vulnerability. Other couples—those who are stuck in the muck and mire of the same old broken relationship—will be attracted to your marriage, as moths are drawn to light. This light of joyful love will motivate others to say, "I want what you have. Where did that come from?"

You can choose love.

You can choose to lean in.

You have all the tools on your pegboard to navigate you safely home.

You can choose to love better sooner. I hope you will.

Finally, my friends, in the words of *Apollo 13*'s Jim Lovell, moments before his team's reentry on their long journey home . . .

"It's been a privilege flying with you."

Toolbox for the Journey

- I need to be filled up, charged up, and energized by the desire to love my partner well.

- Intentional love can be the hallmark of our marriage. This involves developing our conscious awareness of how we are treating others right now. *Right now* is when our marriage is unfolding, and how I treat my spouse *right now* can directly shape our life together.

- No issue will ever be more important than how we communicate our love to one another.

- I am a wounded, needy, broken, selfish person, incapable of loving myself or anyone else perfectly. I am married to [or in a relationship with] a wounded, needy, broken, selfish person, incapable of loving himself or herself or anyone else perfectly.

- Our behaviors are driven by a fear that other people will get too close, or the fear that other people will abandon us. When we can identify our basic fear, intimacy or abandonment, we can begin to learn why we do the things we do—to others and to ourselves.

- Conflict is not a bad thing when intentional interaction can bring healing to the wounds of the past. There can be beautiful possibilities in pain.

- The art of service and sacrifice unfolds in the big and small ways that I can change another person's moment or his or her whole world. By using my gifts and willingness to serve, I can bring about change.

- To delight in my beloved is to release him or her from my expectations. I want my beloved to feel respected, honored, and cherished, not burdened under a yoke of requirements and expectations.

- Conflict is inevitable, but it does not have to be damaging. When we handle the conflict the way God has invited us to, we can engage the conflict instead of the confrontation, and we can tighten and strengthen the bonds of the relationship.

- Lack of information erodes trust. In the absence of information, we write our own stories and create our own truth. Our relationship needs a safe space for each person to speak openly and to feel heard.

- Forgiveness is a muscle that grows stronger with practice, which makes it easier to forgive the next time and the next and the next. The more I forgive, the more I trust that forgiveness is a central part of our relationship, and the more I can trust that you will forgive me when I need it too.

- Anger is a tool for communication. When I can determine the wound that's fueling it, then the anger can calm down and even disappear. Anger is never really the problem, so we must identify what the problem really is.

- The language of connection—*we, us, our*—displays a desire to love well and to find answers that work for both of us and for our relationship together. A person who is speaking the language of connection is listening to truly hear and understand. This can change everything.

- A personal inventory of difficult memories can be very indicative of the people we've become, how we relate to others, and how we engage the world.

- We each need to learn to identify our triggers. With practice, we can begin to learn, recognize, and identify situations that are more triggering than others.

- With effective and consistent consequences, boundaries work.

- We need to recognize our wounds and our brokenness, so we can begin to see how they cause us to act in unloving, separating ways. When we are operating with that kind of humble spirit, then grace and mercy can flow into the conversation. We can choose a path of reconciliation that leads to healing instead of separation.

- Listen first; listen second; listen last.

- The steps of confession and the promises of forgiveness are the glue that keep us together. When a person's heart has changed, then his or her behavior will change as well.

- On a level we may be unaware of, we are attracted to people who trigger our wounds. When our wounds are brought into the light, they can be healed or managed. I believe we are meant to trigger one another's wounds, so they may heal or be managed.

APPENDIX B

Language of Separation v. Language of Connection

Language of Separation	Language of Connection
Uses pronouns: *I, me, you*	Uses pronouns: *we, us, our*
"You're *wrong*!"	"We seem to disagree on this."
"What are you gonna do about it?!"	"How can we reach a solution that satisfies both of us?"
"Well, *you* just need to . . ."	"I think our best move might be to . . ."
"I know . . ."	"I believe . . ."
"I heard what you said, and you said . . ."	"If I heard you correctly, I believe I heard . . ."
"You don't know what you're talking about."	"I believe you are mistaken."
"I know what we should do."	"Perhaps one way to move forward may be . . ."
Is driven by fear	Is based on love
Needs to win	Desires to delight
Protects self	Respects the other person

Language of Separation	Language of Connection
Grasps for control	Seeks to honor
Requires	Cherishes
Is confrontational	Is engaging
Seeks power	Expresses humility
Blames	Seeks to understand one's *own* role in a separation
Interrupts	Allows the other to finish and acknowledges what he or she said
Gets louder	Uses a calm voice
Declarative statements	Asks questions
Makes demands	Makes suggestions
Listens to respond	Listens to hear
Fights over minutiae	Seeks to understand what is important
Long, argumentative texts	Face-to-face communication
Keeps score	Serves
"My perspective is correct."	"I want to understand your perspective."
Hounds the other person for information or answers	Is patient and asks open-ended questions ("Would you tell me more about that?")
Using absolutes: *always, never*	Using qualifiers: *frequently, a lot of the time, often, a majority of the time*
Starts sentences with, "I'm too tired to . . ." or "I'm too busy to . . ."	Says, "I would love to discuss that with you, but is there another time that works?"

Language of Separation	Language of Connection
Says, "I am not the problem," and implies that the other person must be the problem	Responds with, "I can see how I have contributed to this situation," conveying a sense of responsibility for the problem
Is disrespectful and name-calling	Strives to always be respectful in tone and word (the only name-calling that is permissible is a term of endearment without sarcasm)

Acknowledgments

I AM DEEPLY GRATEFUL to the following people:

Tricia Heyer partnered with me, learned my writing voice, and translated my thoughts to the page. Her method offers the best way I could possibly imagine to write a book: I sat with her in coffee shops; I told her my stories, theories, ideas, and experiences with love, marriage, and relationships; and she turned it into a book. Tricia's collaboration carried this book from a pile of notes and ideas into a realized dream in my hands.

Michael Klassen is both a good friend of mine as well as the president of Illumify Media Global. Michael oversaw my master's thesis when I was in graduate school, and he has now overseen the production of this book as well. He is an expert in the field of publishing, and his insights are invaluable.

Dr. Fred Gingrich, a good friend, mentor, and professor at Denver Seminary, has taught me the heart of a counselor. He was gracious and patient during untold hours of lunch discussions about counseling and relationships. I'm thankful for his willingness to advise, critique, and encourage.

Greg Johnson, with Wordserve Literary, made it possible for me to work with Tricia Heyer, navigating the legal and financial side of her collaborative writings. He champions her well, and I am thankful for the partnership with his agency.

Endnotes

1   *Apollo 13*, DVD, directed by Ron Howard (2005; USA: Universal Pictures, 1995).

2   In chapter 18, we will discuss the seven steps of an apology. You can see here that I put all seven steps in one short paragraph. You'll see this really is a lot easier than it sounds. Now you've opened the door for true forgiveness to happen.

3   Chip Ingram and Dr. Becca Johnson, *Overcoming Emotions That Destroy: Practical Help for Those Angry Feelings That Ruin Relaitonships* (Grand Rapids: Baker, 2009), 47.

4   Ingram and Johnson, 50.

5   "The Top 10: The Most Influential Therapists of the Past Quarter-Century." Psychotherapy Networker, 2007.

6   Merriam-Webster, s.v. "compromise," accessed July 23, 2018, https://www.merriam-webster.com/dictionary/compromise.

7   Information in this section is taken from Jay Dee, "The 5 Levels of Communication," Uncovering Intimacy, March 29, 2016, https://www.uncoveringintimacy.com/5-levels-communication.

8   The Seven A's of Confession (Peacemaker Ministries, copyright 1996), adapted from Ken Sande, *The Peacemaker: A Biblical Guide to Resolving Personal Conflict*, 3rd ed. (Grand Rapids: Baker Books, 2004).

9   Adapted from Sande.

10   John C. Maxwell, *The 21 Irrefutable Laws of Leadership: Follow Them and People Will Follow You* (Nashville: Thomas Nelson, 2007).

11   Robert Boyd Munger "My Heart, Christ's Home" (1986), available online at http://navigatorsdetroit.com/MHCH.pdf.